YOU'VE
GOT
CHARISMA!

YOU'VE
GOT
CHARISMA!

Lloyd John Ogilvie

ABINGDON PRESS   Nashville

YOU'VE GOT CHARISMA!

A Festival Book

Copyright © 1975 by Abingdon Press

All rights reserved.

Festival edition published February 1983

ISBN 0-687-47268-7

Printed in the United States of America

To Heather—

no father ever had a better friend, no communicator a more encouraging listener.

CONTENTS

INTRODUCTION

There's a lot of confusion about charisma. We all talk about it; everybody wants it; few know what it is. Leaders seek to develop it, and some religious groups believe they have an esoteric corner on it. Yet there is little comprehension about how it is produced, nurtured, or expressed. It is used to define personality prowess in politics and to identify a person who has the gift of tongues in the swelling ranks of Christians experimenting with the resources of the Holy Spirit. Both groups miss the mark of true charisma. With all this confusion in both church and society about the meaning of authentic charisma, it's time for a clear word about the biblical meaning of this amazing quality. But my purpose in this book is more than clarification; it is to share my conviction that charisma is available to all of us. My title, *You've Got Charisma!* is meant to be more than an attention arrester. It expresses a deep affirmation which arises out of prolonged study and thought.

The outline of chapters follows closely a series of messages about charisma which I have delivered to my Hollywood congregation. Politicians, entertainers, struggling Christians, tired-out churchmen, and the great mass of faithful participants in our church who long for power to live the new life in Christ with joy and gusto have grappled with me to discover the reality of the true charisma of the "grace-gifted" life. This study was prepared with them in mind. As a matter of fact, the progression of thought

developed in response to the tabulation of the needs and
frustrations I heard articulated by my congregation and
people to whom I have listened all over the country. For
them, and for you, I hope that my interpretation of charisma
is more than a simplified universalization and is a
heightened explanation making this power available to all.

The flow of thought in these chapters is arranged in a
progression of insight to illuminate what charisma is, really,
and to communicate how to receive it and grow in its
magnetic potential. I have used a variety of forms of
exposition to get at the central meaning of each of the
biblical texts which undergird the steps in my evolving
understanding. Verse by verse exposition, topical analysis,
and character studies are all used to expose what the
Scriptures say about charisma.

We begin with a study of Romans 12, with an emphasis
on verse six, to find out what it means to be grace-gifted.
Then we will press on in the next chapter to discover the
implications in the charismatic countenance. We all have a
mental picture of a charismatic person as a warm,
life-affirming, positive person. What is this aura of charisma? Why don't more people have it? Can we do anything
with our moods? Those questions will lead us to the heart of
charisma. We will show that the true charismatic personality is developed from within. We will get acquainted with
the needs and potentials of the stranger inside us. Until we
are healed from within, in the heart, there can be no
observable charisma. We will focus on the biblical meaning
of the heart, the inner person, and trace how the Lord
liberates us with grace from within.

Next, our study will lead us to see how the gift of
charisma is expressed in daring dreams and viable visions
of what our life could be as a grace-gifted person. We will
exposit the story of the paralytic by the pool to discover that

one vital gift of the Holy Spirit is creative imagination.

The prayer life of the charismatic person will hold our attention in the next phases of the book. We will dare to ask why we receive so little from our praying. Do we ask unadventuresomely or do we pray great prayers we never expect to be answered? How can we utilize this primary gift of the truly charismatic personality?

The answer is in the power of the resurrection. Christ's resurrection and constantly reoccurring experiences of our own resurrection are the center of the transformation of a person's charismatic capacity. The resurrection is a daily experience, or we are little more than historians looking back wistfully at what God did long ago. The Apostle John will be our example of resurrection living as we trace his experience from his call to discipleship, the crucifixion, Easter, on to his own personality resurrection. Here our style will be varied to expose another form of exposition. A charismatic person is one of the Easter people.

Hope follows naturally. It is the undeniable quality of a charismatic person. We are living in hopeless times. The diminutive gods of our false hoping are dead in America. But what is genuine hope as compared with common hope? We will consider I Peter 1 to show what hope is not and then clarify what true hope is. The questions we will ask are: Do you have hope? Is that hope adequate for life's problems? Can you communicate hope to those around you?

A sign of this hope in a charismatic person is the way he makes the future a friend. We will use the ascension commission to develop the basis of the freedom of charisma. This is the source of a winsomeness expressed in confident trust, excited anticipation, and realization that we will have what we need for each new situation.

In this context, we will move on to a study of the manifold ministries of the Holy Spirit. We will ask ourselves the same question asked by Paul of the disciples of John, "Did you receive the Holy Spirit when you believed?" How we answer determines the source of power for charismatic living.

What does all this have to say about the church as the charismatic community? The early Church was distinguished for mutual sharing. We will try to capture the essence of this by an exposition of Acts 5 and dramatize what happened to Ananias and Sapphira. This passage exposes the strategy of Satan to destroy the Church. We cannot have the Holy Spirit without accountability of the fellowship, nor can we have the fellowship without a mutual sharing of grace.

The final phase of our study spells out the contagion of the charismatic personality. What is the evangelistic manifestation of charisma? We will take a new look at John 15 and the fruit of charisma. In response to the growing concern over evangelism in the church in America, we will search for a fresh understanding of evangelism which is personal, remedial, socially responsible, and reproductive.

There is a new emphasis and excitement today about expository preaching. A book of messages on this central theme of charisma is meant to be of interest to other communicators, but the target is the growing number of readers who need practical help in making sense of the Scriptures for their daily pressures. My hope would be that the same receptivity and gratifying response given to those thoughts in their spoken form would be reproduced now in their revision for the reader.

I am indebted to my assistant, Norma Soll, and secretary, Carmel Buck, for typing the manuscript. They are fellow adventurers and gifts of God to me.

My prayer is that this book will enable you to say, "I've got charisma!"

CHAPTER 1

You've Got Charisma!

I like cab drivers. They have a refreshing way of saying it as it is. What they may lack in understanding of profound issues, they more than make up in colorful language. Recently, while riding across Manhattan, I was the captive audience of a garrulous cabbie. He talked endlessly about the mayoralty race for that mass of humanity we call New York City. After I paid my fare and tipped him appropriately for all his unsolicited advice, he leaned out of his cab window and shouted his last bit of wisdom above the din of the traffic of Madison Avenue. The exclamation may not have been very grammatical, but the truth was undeniable: "Charisma, baby! Charisma! That's where it's at! Charisma's the hope! Some got it; some ain't!"

As he zoomed off and was lost in a traffic jam, I was left to wonder if he understood the profound prognosis for America he had given. Actually, he couldn't have been more accurate and yet more mistaken, all at the same time. Charisma is "where it's at," indeed, but not just as an illusive attractiveness of an admired leader, but as the essence of a quality of life available to all of us!

We hear a lot about charisma these days. We use and misuse it for everything from perfume to politics, yet know little of what it really is or how it is discovered or developed.

For example, a young woman bounced up to me the other evening and said, "I've got charisma! Can't you smell?" She had drenched herself with a new perfume called "Charisma" and was delighted to use this "in" word to describe her condition. The daughter of a friend of mine asked her daddy for a charismatic tennis dress. With understandable alarm, he asked what in the world *that* was. She responded with an esoteric air and read him an ad from *Glamour* magazine: "You can't hold a good look down, not when it's got the real charisma that classic tennis clothes do." Advertisers tell us that you can sell anything from underwear to galoshes if you call it charismatic.

A famous manufacturer of men's suits must have believed this. Its ad in the newspaper was entitled "Charisma Cloth Suits." The ad went on to say, "For the man who is imaginative and innovative and reflects these qualities in his clothes. We design the advanced styled charisma cloth suit. In wool. It's got life. The fabric is woven especially for us in solids, plaids and striping and tailored with look-ahead detailing in the trimly shaped waist, high vent and deeply flapped pockets. Come in and see this handsome example of the American way with wool. It'll give you charisma!"

What is this mysterious thing we call charisma? Some believe that it is the possession of the charmed few. Max Lerner described the popularity of a leading American family: "Beauty, wealth, birth . . . where could you get a better definition of charisma?" But is that charisma? Recently, Rudolph Nureyev tried to identify the reason for his popularity: "I seem to have izuminka, what you call charisma—abnormal drive, nervosity, what people react to violently—they reach out for it, they grab it." We all know people like that. They seem to have a personality power which compels and commands attention; they communicate a confidence and strength. Last week, I heard a man struggling to explain his passionate allegiance to a particular leader, "Don't ask me to explain why I'm for him . . . he's got charisma! Know what I mean?" Most of us would have to plead inadequacy to put into words what he meant, but we would all know what he felt and would like to have for ourselves what he could not explain.

Without understanding what it means, politics has made charisma a must for candidates, insisting that beyond skill and experience, a leader must have this magic quotient. We don't know what we are demanding, but we long for it nonetheless. Self-appointed charismology experts have drawn up long lists of supposedly charismatic leaders and those who, however capable they may be, just don't have it's mysterious powers. But we all want it—and need it!

The story goes that this word was introduced into popular parlance by a scholar for *Fortune* magazine who used it under a picture of John L. Lewis to describe his leadership. *Time* magazine picked it up and made it the "intellectual word of the week." Soon it became a fashionable word to single out particularly forceful leaders who had some hidden power to lead others. Max Weber says that the leaders of history can be categorized as patriarchal, bureaucratic, and charismatic. And our age demands charisma. We want someone with the "savior-of-the-nation charisma" who can enlist and enliven our loyalties.

The fantastic growth of the use of this word is indicative of the need in all of us to push back the boundaries of human inadequacy. As individuals we long for a power, courage, and freedom to live life to the hilt. We want to make a difference where we live and impute new vitality into the people we love. We would like to be able to uplift, encourage, empower people to dare and care. We all want charisma!

But when life forces us to admit our impotence, we search for someone else to rise up and be the spectacular answer to our dreams. As Americans we are sentimental and fanatical about our leaders. We look for personality power to meet the demands of our times, someone whose strength will overshadow our weakness. We all experience the gray grimness of taking ourselves too seriously and our reason for being alive not seriously enough. Have you felt it lately?

Most of us feel it poignantly now in this seemingly leaderless period of history. The present time of crisis in government around the world makes us long for a Churchill, an Eisenhower, or a Martin Luther King to help us sort out the complex issues and blaze a direction out of the morass of blandness. As respected leaders have been exposed and found lacking in moral integrity, as one political party is found to be as confused as another, and as we long for someone in whom we can put our trust and follow, we feel acutely the dependence we have developed on exciting, visionary leaders to fire our blood and impell our allegiance.

Bertold Brecht said, "I pity the nation without charismatic leaders." So say I! But further, I pity any person without charisma. But what we need is what charisma really is—not something to be splashed on or worn or attained or inherited, but realized as a gift. I believe that real charisma is offered to every one of us. That's the good news I have to share.

Richard Lingman ended an article on charisma in the *New York Times* some time ago with an incisive statement: "It is possible that recent revivals of Christianity which seem to employ some of the gifts will restore the word (charisma) to its original meaning. If so, it would be a case of putting Christ back into charisma."

But Christ has never been out of charisma! What we pass off as charisma in unique people today is little more than personality strength or fleeting affinity. *The real meaning of the word is grace-gifted.* Actually, the Greeks originated it. It comes from the verb "to show favor" and is found in Greek mythology to identify the three graces given as gifts of favor from the gods. Paul adopted the word and used it to describe the style of life of a person who has received the grace of Christ. This is the astonishing message of the twelfth chapter of Romans. Here is a portraiture of genuine charisma. Verse six is the pivotal point. Listen to the provocative promise of charisma for all of us: "Having gifts . . . according to grace . . . let us use them." Grace-gifted— life filled with grace—that's what charisma is all about. What goes before and after this focal verse is crucial for us. Paul tells us about the grace which enables charisma and the gifts which express it.

Charisma is motivated, liberated, and authenticated by grace. Paul says, "I appeal to you by the mercies of God." Christ was the incarnation of the mercy of God for him. In the Cross he experienced a love which healed him at the core of his self-justifying, defensive nature. That's where charisma begins—in a gift of an overwhelming sense that we are loved just as we are. There is a winsomeness about people who have been loved deeply. They exude a confidence and chosenness that makes them a magnetic lodestar. We have been called, blessed, confirmed out of unmerited favor. Our healing assurance is that we belong to Christ, and nothing can change that settled certainty. This is not defensive egotism, but the humble acceptance that Christ meant what he said, "You have not chosen me, I have chosen you." This is the steadfast mercy which is the motivating grace of charisma. There is nothing we can do to deserve or earn it, but we can do something to realize it.

On the basis of the grace we have been given, Paul challenges us to present our bodies a living sacrifice. Here the word "bodies" is a composite term to represent our whole life—our natural endowments of talent, training and treasure, the realm of our responsibilities, the people in our lives, our involvements and opportunities—all that we have and are. A charismatic person recognizes that all of life is a gift lent to be spent for Christ. He does not negate his humanity but celebrates it with joy. In response to the grace of Christ, we yield all that we are in a crucial decision of our wills.

J. B. Phillips translates the implications of this vividly. "Don't let the world around you squeeze you into its mold, but let God remold your minds from within." The charismatic person is a Christ-oriented, Christ-possessed person. The false gods of popularity, people, position, power are deposed, and Christ becomes the recognized sovereign of the psyche. From within us he will refocus our values, reshape our personality, and reorient our wills. He will make us like himself. But this is not easy for most of us because, though we may believe in him, our true security and personal identity come from the diminutive gods of our own making at work, in the family, or among our friends. But the truth is this: eventually a man must either sacrifice his idols to his God or his God to his idols! That's the cost of charisma. There is no true charisma until a person can surrender all lesser loyalties to Christ.

I met a friend of mine at the airport the other day. There is an exciting quality about that man. He has purpose and power, a sense of destiny, a winsome freedom, a contagious joy, a capacity to love people creatively and unselfishly, and an involvement in the crucial issues of our time. He is alive with the adventure and drama of life. The sticker marked "occupied" which has been put on his seat in the plane had stuck to the back of his coat. Without knowing it, he had walked through the airport terminal with the bold letters "occupied" across his back. We laughed about it as I tore it from his coat. "Are you occupied?" I asked. Actually, he is; no tag could have described his life more accurately. He is one of those radiantly alive people in whom Christ lives. He is occupied territory. His mind is filled with the mind of Christ, his emotions with the enabling love of Christ, and his body with the vitality of Christ. His resistance and reserve have been broken down by Christ's unchanging love for him, and his psyche has been healed and liberated to be a container and transmitter of the spirit of Christ. He is charismatic.

This is what makes possible the authenticating freedom of charisma. Paul continues, "By the grace given to me, I bid everyone not to think more highly of himself than he ought to think, but with sober judgment, according to the measure of faith." Faith, as abandoned trust, gives us the dynamic honesty of Christ-charisma. The gift enables us to see ourselves as we are and then to imagine what we can become through his power. He gives us a vivid picture of the creative person we can be. We no longer need to pretend or posture. We are free to take sheer delight in the unique creation of love we were meant to be. Self-acceptance and creative self-love flow in an affirmation of life.

The other day I had the difficult experience of telling a woman in my parish that her husband no longer loved her and wanted a divorce. In a moment of real honesty she acknowledged, "Well, I guess it would be hard for him to love me; I don't love myself very much either." We talked at great depth that day and subsequently in counseling sessions. Though she had been a faithful member of the church and had heard the gospel of love for forty-five years, she had never accepted Christ's love for her personally. She

had negated her gifts in a cranky negativism and made her
life and her family's a living hell of judgment and
smothering possessiveness. Then she began to take Christ
seriously. She realized that she did the things she did
because of the person she was. We talked at length about
the power of Christ to change her, and eventually she
accepted his love for her. The results have been amazing.
Rooted in his amazing love, she has begun to affirm herself
and love herself as loved by Christ. The latent capacities of
her personality began to blossom into new tenderness and
warmth. The other day her husband said an astounding
thing. "Will you marry me? I really want to spend the rest of
my life with you!" Her charisma had become an undeniable, irresistible, magnetizing power for new love.

It's important that we expose a contemporary misuse of
the word "charismatic" in a growing group of Christians
around the world. For many of them the term is used for
those who speak in tongues and regard this as the only
undeniable, outward sign that one has received the Holy
Spirit. Recently I was asked, "Are you a charismatic?" I
suspected what the man was asking. "What do you mean?"
I replied. "Well, you know, do you speak in tongues? Have
you had the baptism? You're not charismatic if you
haven't!" Though I believe I have both of these wonderful
gifts by God's grace, I am not willing to relegate this limited
understanding to the term charismatic. There are groups
springing up all over the world using this term. We hear of
the Charismatic Christian Fellowship, the Charismatic
Presbyterians, the Anglican Fellowship of Charismatics,
and a variety of others. Research and investigation into
these groups reveals that the limited use of the term was
never intended by the leaders. Tongues is only one of the
gifts of the Holy Spirit, however liberating and exciting
some of us have found that gift to be. The tragedy of the

misuse of the term is that it segregates and excludes. Grace is always inclusive, and the grace-gifted person is open to all the gifts of the Holy Spirit indwelling in him.

Charisma is not given for our pleasure, but for Christ's purpose. It is equipment for costly caring. Do you want Charisma? Get involved with people and the needs in society; get out on a limb in faithful obedience to the Master; stretch beyond your natural capacities; get over your head in the fast currents of conflict and change; dare to care about the tensions of insecurity and impersonality, loneliness and fear, lack of communication and fulfillment beneath the highly polished surface of the people in your life. Then you will both desperately need and passionately desire power to live a strategic life. And Christ will gift you with capacities which you could never attain or acquire by yourself. Everyone can have his own unique charisma for the particular need of his life. Picture your life—relationships, responsibilities—what do you need?

This leads us to the particular gifts offered for ministry. "Having gifts that *differ* according to grace . . ." This means, I believe, that a special gift will be given for a specific opportunity we have to incarnate his love. It does not mean that we have a permanent endowment of a gift, but rather that when we become engrossed in human need, the gift that is needed will be given to enable us to be effective for him.

"He led a host of captives, and he gave gifts to men" (Ephesians 4:8). What a startling visual image of the charismatic. We are part of the grace-captivated, triumphant procession of released, gifted people who have become equipped to serve. Each gift listed in Romans 12 is an aspect of the portrait of the Living Christ, loving through us. These are offered to all of us. You've got charisma!

First, we are given the gift of prophecy. This is not the

gift of foretelling, but forth-telling. It is the gift of
discernment which equips us to declare the truth in love. It
grows out of the creatively audacious assumption that
Christ can give us the third eye of insight to see what he is
doing at a point of history, the third ear of sensitivity to
listen to what he is saying about what is happening, and the
second voice of compassion to speak his incisive judgment
and mercy. This gift makes us intrepidly daring, bold,
adventuresome, decisive. The gift of prophecy gives the
"man of the hour" charisma so needed today. We are free to
lead out beyond the security of the status quo or the
equivocation of the establishment. Because we have been
set free by grace, we can grasp the jugular vein of any issue
and fearlessly declare the implications of the gospel. We
have a holy abandonment from ultimate loyalty to any
nation, party, political persuasion, company, community, or
institutional religion. Therefore, we can sense what Christ
is doing and join him. Whatever debilitates or dehumanizes
people will be exposed and the truth declared. Prophetic
charisma gives us the courage of Spirit-guided indignation
to step out of the ranks of conformity and speak in
obedience to Christ. This is the charisma of secular saints. I
see this gift manifested in a new power and authority
among Christians today. They become the rallying point for
others to follow. What about you?

This gift of prophecy is inseparable from the other vital
gifts Paul delineates in his listing of the gifts in I
Corinthians 12. In that delineation he precedes the gift of
prophecy with the gifts of wisdom, knowledge, faith,
healing, working of miracles. I believe this is significant. It
helps us realize the prelude to prophecy. Wisdom is the gift
God gives when we come to him and spend time in
conversational prayer with long periods of quiet listening on
our part. When we spread our complexities and concerns

about life and people out before him, we are given his perspective and plan. Knowledge of what is strategic and right flows naturally. We know what we are to do and say. Faith in the Spirit's power to do what he has promised grows within us. We can dare to be obedient to his guidance because we have faithfully left the results to him. The knowledge of what he wants and the faith to believe that it will be done flows into amazing manifestations of healing and miracles we could never have believed possible apart from penetrating, in-depth times of being alone with him.

Ever notice that there are some people who seem to have an incisive insight into situations and a bold expectation of what God can and will do? Trace that prophetic gift back to its source. It will always be the result of profound prayer for wisdom and knowledge. Most of us blunder on leaving a trail of unguided decisions and actions because we have not paid the price of the charisma of prophecy: times alone with our Lord, listening, learning, waiting, growing. We can be given the mind of Christ. A review of our failures of judgment, our misdirection of the people around us, and our ambivalence about life's problems and society's need should alarm us. It drives me back to prayer!

I have people who come to me for advice. As a leader of an institutional church, I am constantly faced with decisions and problems to be solved. As an expositor of the Word, I am continually seeking the implication of what God said in Scripture for what he is saying to me and my people each week. It's a temptation to give quick advice, to make snap decisions, and to blast people in the name of prophetic preaching. I find that when I am open to the Spirit in prayer, I know what to say and how to react. The times I have misfired are usually the result of precipitous judgments, self-propelled aggrandizement, or emotionally induced urgency.

Our families, friends, business associates, church, and community long for charismatic prophecy. We need people who can say, "I believe this is the way God wants us to go." You and I can be that kind of person.

But speaking the truth is one thing; doing it is another. What prophetic insight gives, the gift of service spells out in practical action. Instead of ruminating over the problems of our times, this gift empowers us to dare to pray, "Lord, what do you want me to do?" It asks, "If I loved Christ with all my heart, what would I do at home, at work, in the tensions in the community, in the aching sores of humanity?" This is the charisma of people who love people. It is initiative love that makes the first move to bring reconciliation, healing, and hope, regardless of what others do. This is the charisma of remedial involvement with people and groups. It is impelling, inclusive, sacrificial. This gift earns the right to be heard.

Therefore it is coupled closely with the gift of communication. The gifts of teaching and exhortation belong together. Truth is not just conceptual, it is relational. The charisma of communication is the power of a lucid clarity about what Christ means to us and can mean to others. It frees us to be vulnerable in sharing honestly how Christ can work in the difficulties and frustrations of life. Our failures can become the raw material of a new kind of witness. We build bridges of identification with others by openly exposing our humanity and admitting our own weakness. This charisma has an authentic smell of the earth. People are drawn to it. We all want to find an abundant life. When someone is free to open his life and allow another to see what Christ meant to his personal life, his intimate relationships, his fears and tensions at work, his insecurities about his self-image, then communication rooted in deep communion is experienced.

Inadvertently, exhortation takes place. This is the charisma of spurring another on to the joy of living. We ought to be with people in such a way that they get a fresh vision of their potential. We all know too well how to criticize and condemn. Our own insecurity spills over on to others in limiting negativism. But charisma can be the power of affirmation through us. It builds loyalty and trust. We all need someone in our lives who will affirm our strength and Christ's power to change our weaknesses. What happens to people when you are with them? Are you a liberating or a limiting force, a delight or a drag, a boost or a burden?

I have a friend who is so free of self-consciousness that he has a way of communicating to me a new confidence in myself and courage for my responsibilities. When I have been with him the load is lighter, I am uplifted with a new excitement about being me, I am motivated on to new frontiers of personal growth. He does not put me on or down; rather he is so deeply personal, so open about himself, so concerned about me, that I have the feeling that at that moment I am the only person alive for his attention and affirmation. He has the charisma of communication.

In our church there are small groups called Enabler Groups which meet all over the Los Angeles area. We originated that name for our groups because we have come to believe that the essential task of a Christian is to be an enabler of other people. We are to help people discover how much God loves them, encourage them to take delight in the unique persons they are, free them to maximize the gifts God has given them, and help them discover their parts in his strategy for the world. These groups do just that for the participants. Each is a laboratory of life. A time is given for Bible study, for sharing of needs, and for prayer for each other. The result of learning to enable each other in the groups is that the people have discovered their essential calling in their homes, at work, and in the community. They are no longer uninvolved observers of human problems; they are enablers of the Lord's potential.

Christ wants to make all of us enablers. When we experience the meaning and power of the love of the cross, we are given an enabling ministry. We become partners with our Lord in his creative work in people. Most of us put people off when we think of our task of sharing the faith as a compulsive pressure to straighten out people's thinking, rearrange their lives, give advice, and clarify theology. Not so! We are enablers. What does an enabler do? He affirms people; he is concerned. His major desire is to help others discover how great God has meant them to be. People feel accepted and loved with the enabler. The opportunity to introduce them to the Eternal Enabler comes naturally in that context.

That's what communicating the faith is all about. When the forgiving love of the Cross has healed us at the core, our abiding concern is for the guests God puts in our lives. If conversation, sharing of experience, inquiring into another person's need, patient listening, and liberating empathy are seen in the context of joyous hosting, we will come across as a person others can not resist. They will want to be with us and enjoy our life. A man commented on his conversations and friendship with one of our members, "I don't understand all that he believes, but being with him is like being at a party where he's the host and I am the honored guest!"

This leads us finally to the charisma of dynamic warmth. It is the gift of sensitivity which enables us "to contribute with liberality, give aid with zeal, to do acts of mercy with cheerfulness." The Greek words clarify this gift. We can have singleness of purpose, earnestness, and hilarity. In a world motivated by guilt, we are often inclined to practice the *quid pro quo;* to calculate the effect, return, or result; to fatten people for the kill of our hidden agenda. Contrasted with that, a charismatic person has been freed to become "other-centered"—a man for others. He is free to give himself away warmly. We are able to do this because of the fire of the Spirit burning within us. One of the most vivid New Testament images of the indwelling Spirit in us is fire. This fire purifies our motives, sets us aflame with concern for people, illuminates our life with radiance. Paul crowns the list of gifts with "hilarious mercy." What a great picture of charisma! We are to be the warm, joyous, laughing, loving people who model the difference Christ can make. The world will be able to warm itself by the charismatic fires burning in us.

There is one final gift offered which is not explicitly listed here in Romans 12. But it is the one that makes all the others possible. It is the most difficult gift of all to receive. It's the gift of desire, of a sense of need, of the longing for power to be charismatic. Paul ends this magnificent chapter with a challenge which creates the attitude which opens us to receive. He talks about the kind of love we are to have for others and the world. Let love be genuine; love one another with brotherly affection; bless those who persecute you; repay no one evil for evil, never avenge yourself; overcome evil with good. Who can live that way? No one; that is, no one without the power of the Holy Spirit, the Living Christ. And there's the hope that the promise of charisma will create in us such a sense of our own need, such an awareness of the desperate need of others for grace to be mediated through us, such an urgency about our suffering world that we will accept the gifts offered to us. Jesus said it plainly, "I will make my home in you." Have you invited him to live "at home" in you? If you had five minutes of undivided communion with the Master and he said, "What do you want me to do for you; what gift do you most need to join me in the adventure of healing the world where you live and work?"—what would you say? Be careful how you answer. He takes us seriously and answers by giving us gifts to become involved with him in loving the world.

I asked a startled stewardess on an airplane the other day, "Have you got charisma?" "I don't know! What is it? Is it catching?" she asked. Indeed it is; it's not taught, it's caught from the only true source—Christ himself. Elsewhere Paul summarized charisma and gave us the key, "Christ in you, the hope of glory." If we understand glory as meaning the manifestation of the power of God, then the bold truth is this: Christ in you is the hope of charisma!

In a time when charisma is the most sought after quality, I want to tell you the truth. You've got charisma! It has already been given. The gift is waiting for you.

CHAPTER 2

The Charismatic Countenance

I have a friend who has a charismatic countenance. There is a radiance and a sparkle about him. His eyes shine, and his smile is a passport to immediate trust and confidence. When people are around him they feel the warmth of his mood. He is a dynamic leader because he seldom seems bogged down in moodiness. The outer joy is an expression of an inner experience.

The question I keep asking myself when I'm with him is, Is this man the way he is because of a healthy, sunny childhood? Have things always gone well for him? Has he never known the rough places of rejection of him or his dreams which most of us experience all the time?

My character study of him revealed just the opposite! As a matter of fact, there was a period of his life when he was known for his sour disposition, vile temper, and sullenness. What happened to this man and hundreds of other personalities who have Christ-charisma, can happen to us. They have allowed their experience of grace to flow out in the gift of gracious moods toward life and people.

We'd all like to have a charismatic countenance. No one wants to be a center of doom and gloom. Everyone would like to have an aura of joy, enthusiasm, and pleasantness. But most of us find that we are seldom in the mood. Ah, moodiness! What can we do about our moods?

We all are troubled about what to do with our moods. We too often feel that if we were just better Christians or had more faith we would be joyous all of the time. But we are not. Therefore, one of the most crucial questions about how to live as a charismatic Christian is "What do we do with our moods?"

No one feels gracious all the time. What do you do when you feel down, moody, or "gretzy" as the Pennsylvania Dutch call it? There are times we feel moody regardless of how much we believe in the power of God or would like to be more like Jesus in our hearts, as we were told we should in Sunday school. If we are not to fake a good mood or pretend we never have spells of moodiness, what are we to do? We know how catching our bad moods are. Like a flu virus, they spread through our homes, offices, or among our friends. We would like to have a contagious joy, but that's not always possible. Is there anything we can do to change our moods?

I want to share a working postulate I have tried, and it often works for me. It's based on another line from the twelfth chapter of Paul's Letter to the Romans, "Beloved, never avenge yourselves, but leave it to the wrath of God" (vs. 19). Or, as Phillips translates it, "Never take vengeance into your own hands, my dear friends: stand back and let God punish if he will." This scripture sets out three steps for healing our moodiness: admit, submit, commit. Let me explain this, illustrate it, and see if it makes any sense to you. If it does, then you may want to experiment with it also. Let's approach it scientifically in the laboratory of life and see if it works.

My thesis is this: moodiness is the result of trying to play

God. What I mean is that anytime we assume the responsibility to judge ourselves or other people with condemnatory judgments, a bad mood results. I find it follows almost irrevocably. Before we know it, we are engulfed in an emotion which fits the nature of the judgment. We have the feeling tone of glumness, anxiety, despondency, sulkiness, frustration, self-pity, jealousy, insignificance, competition, dissatisfaction, anger, fear, inadequacy, or sullenness. We muse over our bad feelings, spread our mood, and inadvertently incriminate others because they wonder what they did to cause us to feel the way we do. We end up feeling sorry for ourselves. A spiraling cycle begins, and, like a whirlpool, we are sucked deeper and deeper into destructive introspection.

Judgments are the basis of bad moods. Let me illustrate this with four common breeding grounds of moodiness. Consider first our judgment of ourselves.

We only have to look over the events and conversations of one day to be reminded that we wish we would have said and done things differently. Do you ever say to yourself "Now why did I do that?" or "What an insensitive, foolish, or thoughtless thing to say! There are times I wish I had lockjaw!" Who has not thought or felt that way. We all make goofs or read people or situations wrongly. At times we speak before we think and other times think too long and miss an opportunity to speak when we should. Do you ever think of eloquent, incisive things to say long after the opportunity is past? Of course, we all do. But these are little difficulties which cause us to judge ourselves. What about really crucial decisions, opportunities, and challenges that may never occur again? The "what might have beens" of life trouble all of us. If we could only do it all over again.

A friend of mine has a delightful question she likes to ask:

If you could go back to any point in your life and begin again, where would you choose to start over? What would you do differently? We all would have an answer to that question. But we know that's not possible, and it's just at that point that self-incrimination begins and the bad mood is let out of its cage to stalk about in our feelings. We assume the right to condemn ourselves for what we have done or been, and the bad mood is our way of punishing ourselves in keeping with our self-judgment.

That's just where we take over the management of our little world and play God! Rather than accept God's righteous judgment on the situation, confess our fault, and by grace realize the forgiveness offered to us, we assume the right to judge and punish ourselves. The bad mood of remorse or futility about ourselves results. The punishment seldom meets the crime, and we go deeper and further into a clenched-fisted attitude toward ourselves. We become "up tight."

This is why the Cross was necessary. God knew that we constantly paint ourselves into a corner in self-condemnation. What he did was to provide a way out of the mood which inevitably results. There is no arrogance quite as blatant as the blasphemy of living in a bad mood because we believe that the Creator and Lord of the universe, who could suffer for the sins of the whole world, cannot forgive us. We continue to feel bad because we perpetuate the mood, wishing we had done things differently. God's judgment sets things in focus. Paul uses the word wrath. This is a combination of judgment, love, and forgiveness. God does not wink at our rebellious moods. He penetrates, exposes, and heals the root cause. We can admit our failures and be forgiven. The danger, however, is that the bad mood becomes the habit pattern of our emotional responses, and we fall back into the mood before we know it. We enjoy the costly luxury of a bad mood as if the Cross never had happened.

It's at this point that the scriptural basis of my postulate is helpful. Don't avenge yourselves, but leave it to God. We are not responsible for avenging ourselves. That's God's business, not ours. If we admit our failure, submit to his gracious judgment, and commit ourselves to do whatever love demands to correct in creative restitution the thing we have said or done, then the bad mood or the complex of moods in moodiness will not have to be the inevitable condition of our emotions.

If you are in a bad mood because of self-hate or self-condemnation, then be sure of this—you are playing God!

Now note the way this works out in another cause of moodiness. Often our moods are caused by our physical condition. One of the major causes of this is overexhaustion. What is your body saying to you? Listen; often the body has a clear message that the short circuit of our moods is caused by an overloading of the body. When we overdo or overindulge, we get into a mood which makes us short-tempered, critical, impatient, or anxious. This is the body's compensation for being pressed beyond its endurance. The human ego is basically self-protection. Its job is to stick up for us! It's loyal to us and our welfare. Therefore, when we overinvolve ourselves, there is a natural hostility which grows in us toward life and its demands, and we get moody. Our psyche is protective of our need to rest, recreate, enjoy ourselves, feed both mind and soul with the necessary nourishment. Our bad moods which follow the strain of living are again a condemnatory pattern. We are punishing ourselves for letting life get out of control. We have sacrificed ourselves on the altar of overinvolvement, and the oblation to self is religiously offered. Moodiness follows as our self-inflicted judgment upon ourselves for not taking care of ourselves more responsibly. Again, we have avenged ourselves.

Another breeding ground of bad moods is the people in our lives. When we feel we are offended, neglected, rejected by not being taken seriously, listened to, accepted for what we are, there is an inevitable judgment of people. Then we assume the position of being gods as a means of punishment, in this case not on ourselves, but on others. The mood is usually a manipulative device used to gain or keep control. It is a subtle tantrum. It is a way of trying to get what we want from people when we want it, on our terms. It is an admission of our inadequacy to change our relationships creatively. We realize that we cannot motivate people to do what we want, and the sense of impatience gives illegitimate birth to a sour mood. We cannot communicate our vision for a situation or impress our will for what we think is needed, so we take the only course that's left to us. We brood! The anger which we feel about a person or a group is turned in upon ourselves. There is no creative expression, and therefore we are left to "feel through" our anger within ourselves. We have taken the responsibility of God. Instead of confessing how we feel and leaving the judgment as well as the outcome to him, we have said, "I will repay!" Usually we suffer first, and then others suffer with us because we will not let go of the mood which has grown like a malignancy in our emotions.

One of the most common areas for this is in our families. We all have hidden agenda for the people we love. We want our mates to see things from our point of view and share our values of what's important. When they don't perform according to our standards, we have a mood of self-pity. What about the kids? How we would like to shape them up to life as we envision it! We get angry when they are slow to learn or perpetuate our image. But parents are no less frustrating to young people at times. The reciprocity syndrome goes into action, and they get moody when they do not get their way or don't feel recognition or respect from their parents. The people closest to us are the greatest potential for the danger of trying to run other people's lives.

Environmental conditions can cause bad moods. Frustration is the key cause. When we are not able to adjust our surroundings to meet our expectations, we get frustrated. Frustration is the anxiety of inadequacy of being unable to live within or affect change in the life around us. The lack of time, opportunities, resources, or challenges in a given situation frustrates us. We get urgent to have things arranged to our desires, on our schedule. When they are not, we get impatient. Judgment again enters center stage to play its role of antagonism. Our disappointment with our surroundings starts the mood of discouragement, and soon we are on the way to moodiness. Often we cannot put our fingers on the root cause, but the feelings flow; and soon we are drowned in a joyless uneasiness. We would like to blast out and change things; we yearn to rearrange the status quo and shape it up to our liking. This can be true of marriage, our families, our companies, our community, our church, our world. When we try a reformation program and there is little cooperation or change, we are frustrated. No one sees things the way we do; no one cares as urgently as we seem to; no one follows our direction. We long for the power to rearrange circumstances and people to suit our plans, but there seems to be little lasting cooperation.

In this case the "leave it to God" nostrum of our text does little to help us. Many of us have never learned how to surrender our circumstances to God, discover what he wants to do, and join with him in his strategy, and change things by his power. We run ahead of him, trying to shore things up to our own specifications. We play God over our little kingdom, but no one seems willing to fall down and worship us. We get moody and lick our wounds.

But there is a further cause of bad moods. Perhaps it's the central cause. We get moody because we cannot get God to abdicate rule over us. Many of us are really angry at God. This is difficult for us to admit because of our conditioning. We have just enough Christianity for a fearful but faithless reverence, but not enough to accept his Lordship over us. We wonder if we could not run our universe better than he does. We blame him for what goes wrong with us and our circumstances. We demand that he do something, but there is silence and no change. We send memos of instructions in "prayer" to the universal "front office" but get little assurance that he has adopted our plan. We can agree with the psalmist, "Surely thou art a God who hides thyself." God will not become our attaché to enable our plans. He waits until we are exhausted in our clever scheming and then is willing to give us the plan he has for us, beginning in a relationship of trust and complete relinquishment to him. Omar Khayyam was right, "The worldly hope men set their hearts upon turns to ashes."

The psalmist's question must be answered, "Why are you cast down, O my soul, and why are you disquieted within me?" (Psalm 42:11). Well, what would you say? What is the cause of your moodiness? If the postulate is anywhere near the truth, it is that we have played God in some area of our lives and are filled with a judgment which belongs to God. It's there in the downswing of our emotional cycle that we can do business with the true God whom we cannot mock. Thank God for the winter of emotional feeling when the world seems bleak and frozen. Spring can come if we will allow the love of the Cross to melt us and to give new life to the roots of hope within us.

Now the psalmist's affirmation has meaning: "Hope in God; for I shall again praise him, my help and my God" (Psalm 42:11). That's the only lasting answer to moodiness. When we hope in God we can trust him with ourselves, with our bodies in new reverence for life and health, with people around us in their slowness to change, with our circumstances which we cannot manipulate. When God's in charge we will still have moods. But the difference will be in how long they last. When a man is totally under his command and no longer the judge of himself, others, or life, the moodiness need last only so long as it takes to find the reason and confess it to God. The truth is that we are not in control. Our moods have proven that to us!

John Newton, in my favorite hymn, caught the dynamic nature of the traumatic transition which breaks our moods:

> Amazing Grace! how sweet the sound
> That saved a wretch like me!
> I once was lost, but now am found,
> Was blind, but now I see.

We do not need to perpetuate a wretched mood. The Cross of forgiving grace is offered to us. Admit, submit, and commit!

> The Lord has promised good to me,
> His word my hope secures;
> He will my shield and portion be
> As long as life endures.

That leads me to what I want to talk about next. The charismatic countenance is impossible without getting to an experience of the heart of charisma.

CHAPTER 3

The Heart of Charisma

"Be angry, but sin not; commune with your own
hearts on your beds, and be silent. Offer right
sacrifices, and put your trust in the Lord."
—Psalm 4:4-5

I want to introduce you to a very special person. He is
unique, unlike anyone else here. He has capacities which
are amazing, dreams we should recognize, and powers
which could change our lives. I want you to know this
person, listen to him, honor him. Often, we have neglected
his creativity, debilitated his vision of what we could
become. Frankly, we have stunted this person's growth;
because we have been so busy with another person, we
have not enjoyed his productivity. When we have not been
attentive to his urgings, we have missed what God intended
for us through him.

I want this person to come forward in this service and be
recognized. The purpose of this message is to dignify his
struggle for meaning. He has come to this service with real
needs we often overlook. Now, we dare not mock his
authentic search any longer.

You are probably wondering what famous person I mean.

Some of you who are famous have had a miss in the beat of your pulse because you are concerned that I am going to introduce you without previous warning. Others of you may have suspected that I want to honor a member of the leadership team or some member who needs our recognition. The magnificent but neglected person I want you to meet is none of these!

The person I want you to meet, care for, enable, and encourage is the inner you! Yes, I mean it: the stranger in our midst is the inner person in your hidden, intimate self. He is known only to you and God, sometimes glimpsed at by others, and yet, the most powerful person in your life. I want you to get aquainted with him, liberate and enjoy him. That person lives in your inner heart. It's time to get to the heart of the matter . . . the heart of you!

That's where real charisma begins. Charisma is not a surface attractiveness; it is an experience of the heart which flows through our outer personality and affects the lives of others. We do not seek charisma for itself. It flows out of the wells of the inner self.

The failures and frustrations we have with the person we are with others, coupled with the strains and stresses of our particular period of history, drive us inward. It's there that grace must have its transforming effect, and there the gifts are mediated and experienced. Only then is the result of a charismatic personality manifested.

The psalmist lived in times to match ours. They were times of personal and national calamity. Like us, his problem was how to keep safe in a crazy world. His particular problems related to crop failure, drought, war, and conflict. Added to this was the criticism and expectation of others. Outwardly, life was a mess. That drove him to prayer to cry out to God in the pressure and strain. In the middle of his prayer, he is driven inward. His admonition to

others was a reminder to himself and a secret of charisma
for crises for us. "Be angry, but sin not; commune with your
own hearts on your beds, and be silent. Offer right
sacrifices, and put your trust in the Lord."

That's honest praying. Life had gotten to the psalmist.
But he did not try to wish it away. The words "be angry"
come from expressions that mean being perturbed or
enraged. The Hebrew root suggests the physical accompan-
iments of disturbance and terror.

Ever feel that way? Mass media's instant communication
of the immeasurable muddle of our times jabs at us from
every direction. Added to that are the pressures of too much
to do and too little time. People's problems press in on us;
expectations of others frustrate us. Added to that is the
ever-present realization of what we ought to be and do to be
adequate for a time like this, but we know we are not.

Hans Selye, in his book *The Stress of Life,* talks about the
link between the mind and the body. He calls this link the
general adaptation syndrome. When a person is under any
kind of stress, the endocrine glands react in such a way that
there is a general "alarm reaction." Anger and fear cause
the adrenal cortex to secrete more adrenalin into the blood
stream than usual. This enables us to react quickly and
have greater endurance. But other glands become involved.
When the cause of stress is not removed, the alarm reaction
continues for about twenty-four hours. At this point the
body goes into what Selye calls the "stage of resistance,"
which may continue almost indefinitely. We do not return
to normal, but a constant stream of hormones mobilizes the
resources of the body against the cause of the stress.
Outwardly we may appear normal in spite of the inner
battle for stability. It's the same reaction which would come
from a sublethal dose of poison, suffering from too much
heat or cold, lack of sleep, overworking, or some physical

catastrophe around us. In each case the same process goes on in the body, using the same glands. Often something breaks down under the strain of the chemical imbalance in the blood stream. That's usually the weakest part of the body. Thus, every organ of the body, and some more than others, is affected by the horrendous disturbance of our daily lives.

I believe that many of us live with a constant alarm reaction going on in our bodies. One crisis is matched by a greater one, and even when we get things sorted out in our own lives for a brief time, someone else is usually ready to jab us with a problem which keeps us agitated. Our society, our present turmoil in government, and the unbelievable cruelty we see around us or on the TV set, never allows our bodies or our minds to return to normal.

That's the condition the psalmist's word anger exposes. It's more than a temper tantrum; its an agitated physical and emotional condition. We are in a constant state of shock. We all feel it: danger in a violent world; demands from a multiplicity of pressures; deadlines; fear of failure; demands of people; distortion between what we want and what we can produce.

But there is an answer. The psalmist found it. There is a capacity of the spiritual life which I want to call the adaptation syndrome of the heart. It too has an alarm reaction and feeds needed power to meet the crises and pressures. But instead of agitation, it infuses peace. The source of this energy is in the heart, the inner person we need to meet and care for.

"Commune with your own hearts . . . be silent." There it is: a crucial part of prayer is communing with our own heart. In the Scriptures, the term "heart" is used to describe that inner dimension of human personality which is a combination of intellect, emotions, and the will. It's that

part of us which is known only to us and God, which is the
point of contact with the Holy Spirit. The heart was created
to be the reservoir of the Spirit. When Jesus spoke of the
indwelling of the Spirit he said, "Out of his heart shall flow
rivers of living water" (John 7:38). He was immensely
concerned about what's in our hearts. He identified himself
as the one who searches the heart. Those who want to see
God must be pure in heart, single in their desire to do his
will. He alerted people to the uncleansed heart as the real
source of evil action. And he warned us that our hearts will
be given over to whatever commands our allegiance:
"Where your treasure is, there will your heart be also."

Clearly Jesus recognized the inner and outer dimensions
of personality and identified the heart as the most crucial
source of what we do and become. Paul said that response
to Christ required both. "If you confess with your lips that
Jesus Christ is Lord (outward) and believe in your heart
(inward) that God has raised him from the dead, you shall
be saved." To believe with the heart is to marshall all inner
memories and guilt, all the needs and drives, all the hopes
and expectations for the future, our self-image, our plans
and purposes, and commit them to Christ. That's the
beginning of charisma. In that hidden recess of our inner
being we are the real person who needs the love, forgiveness, and healing of the grace which is the core of
charisma.

When only our outer life has been touched by grace,
there is a brief flush of excitement, but no lasting change.
When we see situations and people we have trusted to our
Lord to change and find an answer, we are delighted, but
the excitement fades. When we ask for help in our
problems and receive God's intervention, we are thrilled,
but later in our aloneness, we feel strangely disappointed
with the same old person who lives in us. The Christian life

is a swing of ups and downs, enthusiasm and despair, spiritual highs and lonely lows.

That's why I want us to learn to love that inner person as much as our Lord does and allow him to do his creative work there. That's the only alternative to constant stress and strain outwardly in life. "So we do not lose heart," Paul said. "Though our outer nature is wasting away, our inner nature is being renewed every day" (II Corinthians 4:16). The inner power meets the outward pressure!

When we commune with our own hearts, we draw from the inner resources of Christ's indwelling power. But also we gain direction from the convictions, goals, and true desires Christ has for us which have become our heart's desire. Courage comes from that. I believe that the sickness of our time, the personal problems of our lives, and the psychological illness which is everywhere is the result of the division between what's in our hearts and what we do. The distance between our true and projected self is the breeding ground of emotional tension and agitation.

Mark Schorer's analysis of Sinclair Lewis points up what I mean. "In flight from himself, he tried to compensate by his immense vaudeville talent. He never got around to connecting his talent and his life so that he knew who he was. There was no inner certainty, no balance, no serenity, nothing between heaven and earth to which he could withdraw for quietude and healing. Because he never knew himself, he outraged himself."

That may seem a bit severe. But listen to Lewis about his own life. "I spent my life doing neither what I ought or what I wanted." That sounds like a friend of mine who commented, "Every step I take is a struggle between what I am and what I ought to be!" Shakespeare was near the truth in *Measure for Measure,* "O what man may within himself hide, though angel on the outward side." For all of us, the problem is that doing usually precedes being. John Steinbeck's Ethan was right, "Men don't get knocked out, or I mean they can fight back against big things. What kills men is erosion: they get nudged into failure." That's because there are no moorings in the heart, no criterion beyond people's opinion, no motive greater than daily schedule demands. What e. e. cummings concludes as his advice to those who would write in *The Magic Marker* is universally true: "To be nobody but yourself in a world which is doing its best, night and day, to make you everybody else—means the hardest battle which any human being can fight, and never stop fighting."

But what if you don't know the inner person very well and therefore have never befriended and defended the true person you want to be? We are told a maxim these days to love ourselves, that you can't love anyone until you love yourself. But how can we love a person we have never taken the time to know?

Who is this stranger inside of us who needs befriending? What is he like? What parental conditioning has made him the way he is, what guidelines formed his superego or conscience, what hurts debilitated him, what successes nourished his agenda of what he likes? Wouldn't it be great if we could say of our inner person what Sherlock Holmes said of Dr. Watson? "You are my one fixed point in a world of change." Or what Lincoln could say in the midst of criticism and conflict. "I desire so to conduct the affairs of this administration that if at the end, when I come to lay down the reins of power, I have lost every other friend on earth, I shall have at least one friend left, and that friend shall be inside me." Do you feel that way about the person inside of you?

Most of us would have to respond, "Well, I don't know, I'm not that well acquainted with him to know!" The psalmist's admonition is on target—meditate with your own hearts in silence. Get quiet enough to listen to what you're like inside, and then ask God to integrate and liberate that inner friend.

Jesus said, "If thine eye be single, thy whole body shall be full of light." In the context of what we have been saying the heart is that eye of spiritual sight. If it is single, unified around the gracious Lordship of Christ, our whole being will know the truth, and we will have the power to do it. Trench was right, "Lord, what a change within us one short hour spent in thy presence will avail to make."

What does the Lord do through grace in the time of communion within? First he speaks tenderly his personal word of grace. "I love you. You are accepted. You are mine." Let those words water the dry, hard places within. Then he goes on, "I know all about you. I remember all the times this inner person was bruised when you could never let anyone know. I felt with you the blows and cuts to your feeling O.K. Let's take each one of those memories and let me heal them with forgiveness." Then, from within us he points us to the feelings we have about people. One by one he gives us his perspective of tender love. Now our personality structure is dissected under his careful penetration. "Why do you act and react that way?" he asks. There is affirmation of our growth and correction of all the feelings and patterns which are not in keeping with his life and purpose for us. Then he begins to take us back over his message, and we are forced to see our cherished ideas, beliefs, and presuppositions which form our values, political persuasions, and prejudices. We are amazed at the inconsistencies, but also assured by some of the growth in our thinking. Now he flashes our commitments before us. What do they have to do with the kingdom of God? We know we could never change them without a time like this with him. "But what's going to happen to me?" we ask desperately. "Where is my life leading? What will I become?" Then he helps us picture our outer life under his control, ourselves in his image. Listen to him! "I will give you enough guidance for each day! I will guide you in each decision. You will have enough wisdom, energy, and clarity for each situation. But come back here in quiet with me each day, and I will paint the picture of the next steps, help you feel through how to react. I am in you always; when things get tough just trust that I will shoot into your mind what to think and into your mouth what to say!"

There is no true charisma without consistent times like that. The other evening before I went to sleep, I read a portion of Scripture and prayed quietly. What was intended to be a brief end of the day prayer went on for a long time. I withdrew into the inner chamber. The defenses were down. In the quiet, I saw some things about my life which I could never have learned from anyone else. I saw that I was being unfair to one of my children. I would never have accepted anyone's advice about that. Then a picture formed in my mind of a conversation with this child. I could not believe what I saw! I was reacting and expressing myself in a way that turned the child on to me. We were close and open to each other. Most of all, I was listening. The prayer closed by the Lord saying to me, "Now that's the way I will relate through you tomorrow." And he did.

There are times I do what I call a swing-around in quiet prayer. I literally allow my mind to swing around to all the people of my life, all my responsibilities, my problems, and my unresolved decisions. It takes time, but oh, the time it saves in my outward life! What Whitehead said of moral education is also true of daily guidance. It is impossible without the "habitual vision of greatness."

This leads to the third aspect of the reminder the psalmist

gave himself and admonition he gives to us. "Offer right sacrifices, and put your trust in the Lord."

But what's a "right" sacrifice? Our minds shoot to Psalm 51:16-17: "For thou hast no delight in sacrifice; were I to give a burnt offering, thou wouldst not be pleased. The sacrifice acceptable to God is a broken spirit; a broken and contrite heart, O God, thou wilt not despise."

A broken and a contrite heart is one that has been battered by the failures of self-effort and human failure. A contrite heart is one that confesses and accepts forgiveness. Once we have communed with our Lord in our own hearts in silence, we know that we have done what only grace could atone. Contriteness seeks his guidance and direction. Arrogant self-determination; mixed, unpurified motives; distorted relationships; grandiose purposes are all tempered, melted, and recast in the fires of his consuming love. All he wants from us is the sacrifice of our hearts—an inner person completely given over to his control. Is that too much to ask? Especially in the light that he knows what's best for us, can give meaning to the muddle of our lives, and can give power to help us meet life's pressures. Only that can change what Thoreau called "the quiet desperation of our lives."

I like John S. Dunne's poem "A Search for God in Time." He tells us that there is a time for everything in life—a time to live and a time to die; a time for despair and a time for confidence; a time for action and a time for reflecting; a time for youth and a time for old age. But most especially, there is a time to remember God and a time to wait for him.

That's where charisma is born and nurtured. J. Douglas Brown in his outstanding book *The Human Nature of Organizations* analyzes the attributes of an effective leader. Though he is writing for the business organization, what he says is true for all of us and affirms what I have been trying to say here. Building on the basic attributes of introspection, he says:

> The understanding of self which comes with introspection
> provides the responsible leader with one of the most fundamental attributes of effective leadership—integrity. In the meaning
> here intended, integrity implies that a person has developed,
> over time, a consistent ordering of his systems of values,
> attitudes, and goals. In common terms, he has come to know his
> own mind, conscious and unconscious, and for what he stands
> and for what he will fight. In the effective leader, this kind of
> integrity is not alone a moral or intellectual qualification for
> appointment. It is an attribute functionally prerequisite to
> continuing effectiveness in directing day-to-day operations in
> human organization.

Closely related to integrity in Brown's thinking is
intuition. This he defines as the capacity to feel what's right
in a particular situation drawn from more than logic,
experience, or convictions. Note the progression: introspection, integrity, intuition. Out of these comes what Brown
calls a leader's style. This is the clarity of his mind and
expression, sustained enthusiasm, sympathy, courage,
wisdom, originality, humor, sensitivity, and cultural refinement. "However style is expressed, it must be the
visible manifestation of a unique personality."

The same is true of authentic Christian charisma. It is
begun in the heart through introspection—communing
with your own heart, prayer; it is empowered through
integrity, the unification of the facets of mind, emotion, and
will around the mind of Christ; it is expressed with intuitive
sensitivity—guidance through the Holy Spirit for each
moment's reaction and decision; it is exposed in a
style-graciousness rooted in a broken and contrite heart-
loving, bold, courageous, daring.

The greatest gift we can give the people around us is time with our Lord alone. There'll be no charisma from us for them without it. The inner computer of our being will have no memory factors to react to the pressing questions of our time. We will wabble under life's demands. The outer forces will collapse us until we have an equalizing force within.

That's the heart of the matter—the heart of charisma!

CHAPTER 4

"Well, What Did You Expect?"

"Well, what did you expect?" is a question we ask someone when he has faced a disappointment we feel he should have anticipated. We also ask it when someone is amazed at an unexpected joy. It's a good question for anyone who wants charisma. I believe that God is more ready to make us charismatic than we are to ask. Prayer for charisma is not to overcome God's reluctance but to grasp his unlimited resources. It's his idea, you know! He creates in us the desire for what he is prepared to give. The real question then is "What do you expect?"

When I began my ministry in Hollywood, it was a moment of tremendous expectation for me. Everywhere I went I heard of the church's expectations for its new pastor. A friend of mine said that when a pastor accepts a new call he becomes a lame duck where he is and a rumor where he's going. My schedule in Bethlehem after I was called contradicted the first part of that and, by everything I could sense in Hollywood, verified the second part.

Many people have spoken to me about their concern over this expectation. They are troubled that the expectation is too high—that no man could ever fulfill it. But then, I, too, have expectations. I am filled with expectations for the congregation, for myself, for our life together, for the next steps of God's strategy the church. For that, others have cautioned me. "Don't set your expectations too high!" they have advised. "Remember, they are just human beings, and they will disappoint you if you expect too much."

One day in my quiet time, I asked God about these expectations and the concern people were expressing about them. As I waited and listened intently for his guidance for me, suddenly a rushing flood of Scriptures inundated my mind, drowning any lingering fear or doubt. Strange and wonderful, isn't it, how Scriptures memorized years before become God's fresh Word to us? It was as if I had heard them for the first time. They were the Word of the Lord for Lloyd—and now I pray for you. Listen.

> "Behold, I am doing a new thing: now it springs forth, do you not perceive it?" (Isaiah 43:19)

> "Then I saw a new heaven and a new earth." (Revelation 21:1)

> "What no eye has seen, nor ear heard, nor the heart of man conceived, what God hath prepared for those who love him." (I Corinthians 2:9)

> "O, sing to the Lord a new song." (Psalm 96:1)

> "For the love of Christ controls us, because we are convinced that one has died for all; therefore all have died. And he died for all, that those who live might live no longer for themselves but for him who for their sake died and was raised. From now on, therefore, we regard no one from a human point of view; . . . therefore, if any one is in Christ, he is a new creation; the old has passed away, behold, the new has come." (II Corinthians 5:14-17)

As I thought and prayed about this, I was set free by a liberating conviction. Our problem is not that our expectations are too high. The common debility which you and I share is that our expectations may be too low, too small, too inadequate compared to God's expectations. The real question is not "What *did* you expect?" but "What *do* you expect?" Based on God's promises, what do we expect?

However great your expectations might be for me, they are mediocre in comparison to what God is ready and willing to do in my life if I will abandon myself completely to him; and if I were to paint the bold brush strokes of my most adventuresome vision for my congregation, I would barely begin to characterize the amazing portrait of the exciting plans God has in mind for them.

You see, the crucial thing is not a church's expectation of your pastor or his for his new congregation. The important issue is our combined expectation of God based on the dimensions of the dream for us he places within us. I have come to believe that praying begins with God. He initiates within us a desire to pray for the very thing he is more ready to give than we are to receive. Praying is not so much convincing God but boldly claiming his readiness. The dream for the future begins with him, sweeps down into the heart of man, and then is returned to him for his clarification and direction. An undeniable manifestation of our commitment to Christ and the outer sign of his indwelling power in us is our capacity to be indefatigable in our expectations, based not on human adequacy or skill, but on his unlimited resources of power.

But how often we are surprised, amazed, by the breakthroughs of God. Often we are like the man who went to the pool of Bethesda for thirty-eight years with religious consistency, but did not expect really to be healed. His ritual of evasion debilitated his expectation. The truth of the matter is that he no longer expected to be healed. Perhaps, he no longer wanted to be healed! Healing would mean responsibility and implementation and accountability.

The man by the pool is like many of us who pray our prayers, attend church, participate in Christian groups, study the Bible and practice our piety, but do not expect a miracle. But the same Lord who broke the barrier of human sin on the Cross comes to each of us, as he came to the man by the pool of Bethesda and asked, "Do you really want to be healed?" In other words, he was asking the man if he wanted to be different, if he wanted God's dream for him, if he could envision what God could do with his life if he trusted him?" What a question! What lack of empathy would have caused Jesus to ask such an unkind and unthinking question?

We can feel as well as hear the response of the man's paralyzed spirit. "Do I want to be healed? I have been carried here thirty-eight years for healing—fourteen thousand, two hundred and seventy days! And you ask me if I want to be healed! I, who have never known the fulness or joy of living; I, who have been shut up in this horrible living death; I, who have had to sit and listen to the hypochondriacal talk of the other invalids; I, who have suffered in this gnarled body, unable to walk, frightened to move for fear of pain; I, who have known nothing of the excitement of healthful energy vitalizing my being; I, who have waited for the waters to be troubled by the angel so that I could be the first one into the healing waters of the pool to be healed; I, who am always pushed aside by someone else who appropriates the healing power before I can; I, whom no one will put into the water and, therefore, am left in painful paralysis forever! And you ask me, 'Do I want to be made whole, healed?' What an absurd question! Of course I want to be healed! Would I be here if I didn't?"

It sounds like a rather insensitive question, doesn't it, when you look at it that way? Why did Jesus ever ask a question like that? Jesus knew that this man's need was for spiritual breakthrough and that for him this was indeed the central question.

Do I mean that perhaps he no longer really wanted to be healed? This is exactly what Jesus suggests. Yes, though he had been carried there for thirty-eight years by his friends and family, there is now a serious question as to whether he wanted to be healed, for he could rest day by day in the quiet shade around the pool and talk to his friends about his sickness. No longer did he have to work out in the blasting sun like others. All of life was introverted in on himself. All conversation with others was about himself and his own needs and that magical day when, finally, he would be different and healed. It never occurred to anyone to stop and question whether he would be interested in being healed or not. Only Jesus could see underneath the surface of this man's pretense, to realize that in his prostrate position he was huddled against God, hiding from reality. Jesus made it possible for this man to see that he was not really sincere any longer.

As we come to the sanctuary for the healing of our needs, the fulfillment of our expectations, and the experience of charisma, Jesus meets us in a disarming encounter and asks, "Are you quite serious? Do you want what you ask? What kind of a church do you want to be? What do you want to have happen in your lives and the life of your church? What do you dare to dream I can do with your life? Do you really want my purpose and power for you? Do you want to love others as I have loved you? Do you want a Christian marriage? How important is my will for your society? Do you want to learn how to communicate your faith to others? Do you want to live out your faith in your work? Do you want to be a new creature in my love? Is that what you want? Is that why you have come?"

And we say with the man by the pool, "Why Lord Jesus, of course we want it! We want that more than anything else in the world!" But then he says, "Do you really?"

There is great significance in the fact that the man had been by the pool for thirty-eight years. John selected from the treasure chest of the miracles of Jesus those that particularly incarnated those truths he sought to proclaim: Jesus, the beginning of a new age—the transforming of water into wine at the marriage of Cana; Jesus, the truth of God—the encounter of truth in him with the woman by the well; Jesus, the light of the world—the blind man is healed and says, "Once I was blind and now I see!"; Jesus, the Resurrection and the Life—Lazarus raised from the dead. Now here in this passage John asserted that Jesus was the hope of paralyzed Israel which had wandered in the wilderness for years unable to accept the blessing of the Promised Land because of unwillingness to claim the promise of God that he would go before them from all enemies. When Jesus healed this poor paralytic he was saying to all Israel, paralyzed in external legalism and powerless piety, that it, too, needed to be healed. Why did he choose this one man out of the uncountable sea of wretched humanity beside the pool? He had more than the healing of this one man in mind. He had the healing and renewal of Israel focused in this man.

I am convinced that the length of time Israel spent in the wilderness was calculated by their reluctance and not by God's timing. The Promised Land lay waiting, but they could not go in and possess the land because of lack of daring trust in the Lord who had led them out of Egypt, who had gone before them by day in a pillar of cloud to lead them along the way, and by night a pillar of fire to give them light. But notice further in that Exodus account (Exodus 13:22): "The pillar of cloud by day and the pillar of fire by

night did not depart from before the people." I have often
wondered how often the Lord must have led them up to the
Promised Land. How very gracious of him to lead them
again and again, with interceding, innovative guidance to
weave strength into the thin thread of their trust in him.
When they finally reached the border of the Promised Land,
they paused. Why? They asked, "Is it possible to possess the
Land?" It's almost as if they had become secure in their
wandering rather than in God's promises. He had shown
his power—why did they hesitate? They had been in
bondage for nine generations to the Egyptians and in
bondage to fear for forty years of wandering.

I believe in group process and committees, but I am not
very impressed with the committee which was appointed to
spy out the Promised Land. Their report was accurate. The
land was flowing with milk and honey. Caleb had the
courageous minority vote. "Let us go up at once and possess
it; for we are well able to overcome it." But the majority
report was less courageous: "We are not able to go up
against the people; for they are stronger than we. . . . And
all the people that we saw in it are men of great stature. . .
And we seemed to ourselves like grasshoppers" (Numbers
13:30-33).

"Seemed to ourselves"—did you catch that? It's what we
are in our own sight that makes the difference. But is our
picture of ourselves, our church, God's picture? That makes
an even greater difference.

The painful truth is that we can become so obsessed with
difficulties that we cannot see God's dream for us.

A charismatic person is one who is focused on the picture
of what he is and can become through God's grace. But I
have found that I must reclaim that grace every day. I often
get obsessed with problems and lose sight of the dream.
Then I feel I must work my way through the problems to

recapture the vision. This is nothing other than self-justification. In times like that I feel my Lord near with the tender but firm words, "Lloyd, give me those problems. Allow yourself to be my problem. Start right now where you are with what you are. Leave the rest to me."

At that moment everything hangs in balance. Do I want to be healed? Do I want a fresh flow of grace? Or do I want to try to work it out myself? One way leads to an up-tight stiffness in my personality and strain in my relationships. The other leads to freedom and new charisma. When I accept his uplifting hand, the dream becomes clear again. The result is always that I feel that the best years are ahead for me. That's a sure, undeniable test for me—when I feel more excited about the future than the past.

What about you? Is the best still ahead? What about our church? Have we had our finest hours, or are they still in the future? What about the Christian enterprise in our nation? Is God about to write a new chapter in the book of Acts, or are we in a post-Christian era as some suggest?

I am always disturbed by the account of Jesus' visit to his home town of Nazareth. We are told that "he could do no mighty work there because of their unbelief." We have the awesome power to limit God! William Barclay put it clearly: "There is laid on us the tremendous responsibility that we can either help or hinder the work of Jesus Christ. We can open the door wide to him, or we can slam it in his face."

But there are times when we miss God's dream, he disturbs us with a nightmare to alert us to our sin against the future. We are like Zechariah who sat bold upright in bed, awakened by a nightmare which gave him a cold sweat. What he could not handle in his conscious mind, God dramatized in a spine-tingling dream. In the year 520 B.C. he had gone to bed with a troubled spirit. What was

wrong with him? He had returned to Jerusalem with his
family and a group of exiles. Cyrus had released them from
Babylon in 539. They returned to Jerusalem to rebuild their
homes, the Temple, and the walls of Jerusalem. It was not
long, however, before they began to take their signals of
guidance from the culture around them, rather than from
God. Enthusiasm waned, and building operations dwin-
dled. They were harassed by the Samaritans, crop failure,
indifference, growing secularism, and skepticism.

Zechariah internalized the problem of his people. He felt
the reconstruction of Jerusalem on his own conscience. He
was a sensitive, God-led man who could not rest while
others gave in to despondency and discouragement.

No wonder he had a nightmare which woke him in a cold
sweat! He had eight successive dreams. The third dream
seems to be most crucial and is most applicable to us. It is
the nightmare of all ages and declares a truth desperately
needed in our time as individuals, a Church, a denomination, and a nation.

Zechariah dreamed that he saw a young man with a
measuring line in his hand. He asked him where he was
going. "To measure Jerusalem, to see what is the breadth
and length." Then in the dream, two angels came forward
in urgent response to the young man's answer. They were
deeply concerned and challenged Zechariah.

"Run, say to that young man, Jerusalem shall be
inhabited as villages without walls because of the multitude
of men and cattle in it. For I will be to her a wall of fire
round about, says the Lord, and I will be the glory within
her."

They were so concerned with the man's obvious inten-
tions with the measuring line that they wanted Zechariah
to stop him before he committed the debilitating sin of
underexpectation. He, the representative of most of his

contemporaries and so many of us, was sinning against the future.

And what was this sin? Simply this: he was going back to measure the Temple and Jerusalem on the basis of previous measurements before the exile. He wanted to rebuild out of reverence for the past, but without vision for the future. He had learned nothing from God's purging and judgment in the exile. Now, still trusting in himself and his own vision for the past, he wanted to duplicate what was without consideration of God's expanded vision for his people. He wanted to establish the old securities and settle back into a Jerusalem of old.

The answer of the Lord's messenger can be understood in three aspects which touch us deeply. They portrayed a different kind of life than the traditions which the proud, self-satisfied, self-perpetuating Jews had known. The Lord's message depicted an astounding new life of freedom. He now offered his people a new life without limits, without defenses and without frustration. God's new measurement would be beyond preconceived boundaries, without walls of defense, and his glory would be their only security.

Could it be that we, too, just like those postexilic Jews, have taken the wrong measurements of our Jerusalem? Let's consider our Jerusalem to be ourselves, our family, our job, our community, our world. Ever find that you are living with an old idea of yourself and others, even after the new life has begun? Christ has set us free from the bondage of sin and selfishness and yet we go on measuring our lives by the old measurements. Like the man with the measuring line, we sin against the future by thinking of it on too small a scale. God has called us to a life without reservations. Yet how many of us are boxed in by inadequate measurements?

It's good for all of us to go back to our home town every so often. But not for long! The womb of memory gathers us up in security and solicitousness. The pressure to grow and adventure is off for just a moment. We can stand still in the quiet of what used to be. Then we can remember, but not for too long! One of the startling conclusions which comes to us is how different our conceptions of life used to be. How small our measurements were then! How easy it is to fall back into the security of old dreams easily fulfilled and escape the creative pressure of the Spirit to move on.

Too small!

Your measurements are too small!

Old measurements in a new life!

True for you? The daring, adventurous, life-changing, world revolutionary faith of a God who moves mountains seems rather illusionary when we return to our true self, our old patterns, the same old family, same old measurements.

As a man thinketh, so is he! What do you really think about yourself, your friends, your job, your spouse, your children, the church? Without a vision the people perish. Don't forget Joel's promise. The gift of the Holy Spirit will mean "young men shall see visions and old men shall dream dreams. I will pour out my Spirit, and they shall prophesy."

A few weeks ago, I spent the afternoon with a friend who was in the binds of indecision about the future of God's strategy for his life. I asked him a question. "If you knew that the limitless power of God were available to you, what would you do?" His response was, "Why, that changes everything! That puts it into a whole new perspective. What a difference!" We talked at length in that ambience of viable vision and then covenanted with each other to pray that God's dream would become true for us. On the long drive home he had time to think and pray. This is what he wrote me some days later: "On the way home yesterday, I had about two hours to do nothing but drive and think. I had a dream, and you have taught me to be open enough to tell you what that dream was. I think that it is a presumptuous dream. I don't know what could ever happen, but that's the way the dream came out. I have claimed it for the glory of our Lord!" He's on the way!

I'll never forget a clergyman in the South who was bottled up with frustrations and reservations. He had all sorts of resentments and bad memories crammed down in his psyche. He was becoming what he was hiding. I am convinced that only the things we hide are the things which can hinder us. In the conference we attended together he was encouraged to excavate the garbage and allow our Lord to incinerate it in a consuming fire of forgiveness. We talked late into the night and then prayed together. After the cleansing process was over, I asked him, "Now what are your dreams for the future?" Released from the tension of the maintenance of his internal garbage dump, he could see his family and church from God's perspective and potential.

But our dreams must pass through the narrow door. They must be purged and refined, refocused and redirected. This is why we need each other. It is in deep fellowship that we deal, not only with the conceptual faith, but also encourage and enable each other in Christ-centered, Cross-oriented dreaming.

It is in honest, open fellowship with trusted fellow dreamers that we can ask:

1. What would your life be like if you were completely surrendered to Christ?
2. Have you ever relinquished your own control of the future and all its hopes and wishes to him?
3. If you were free of reservations and preconceptions, what is the maximum dream Christ has for you? Is it an extension of love; will it stand the test of the Cross?

Does it will the ultimate good for others and the situation? Will it upbuild the kingdom in every way?

4. And lastly, is there anything in you standing in the way? A problem is only that which stands in the way of claiming and experiencing God's goal for us.

In the light of that, what is your boldest dream for your life, the people you love (and a few you may not love!), and your church?

But like the paralytic beside the pool, "now" may be too soon for some of us. We are like the crowds who cheered the tight-rope walker who was about to walk across Niagara Falls with a wheelbarrow. The people cheered and encouraged him on. Then he turned and said, "Some one of you get into the wheelbarrow!" Jesus does that, all the time. How much do you want to be healed? Do you really want my dream?

I remember talking to a scratchy, negative, up-tight, Presbyterian agnostic who was critical and angry about his church. If hostile judgments, noncontextual proof texts, and pious put-downs could have changed his church, his would have been a slice of the millennium. So I asked, "Are you willing to pray, 'Change my church beginning with me'; to seek to be what you envision others ought to be; to love with affirmation in order to help people change?" That was more than he bargained for.

But countless others march before my mind's eye. These are part of a new kind of Christian for our time. One man stands out in particular. He decided to call a moratorium on the paralysis of analysis of what might have been in his church and started a one-man crusade of love in his church. He began to meet weekly with his pastor for sharing of needs and mutual, supportive prayer. He asked God for a few others with whom he could meet and share the adventure. The contagion of his love spread throughout the church. One man, plus the Lord, was a majority for the beginning of a new church.

Or I recall a woman whose whole security had grown around her criticism of her family. Everyone in her life was unsettled by her coercive criticisms. People tried especially hard to please her, only to find new criticism in another area. When life fell apart for her, she confessed her terrible insecurity. I asked, "What if people became what you demand, would you be different?" "No," she responded, "I guess I had hoped that if people did what I wanted, that would be a sign of love." Only Christ could give her that love, and when she received him, the cankerous judgments fell away like scales from her eyes. Christ healed her obstacle obsession by lifting her attention away from her negative judgments to the Cross and his unchanging love for her. What a difference there is now in her home, her church work, her efforts for social justice in the community.

One of the places I go to recapture God's dream is back to one of my favorite scriptures. It's in that magnificent third chapter of I Corinthians. The Corinthians were running out of power and vision because they were enjoying the unenjoyable luxury of divisiveness and party spirit. Paul breaks the bind of their impotence in a stirring way. He reminds them of their purpose, power, and potential. "Do you not know that you are God's temple and that God's Spirit dwells in you?" That always reorients my perspective on the reason I am alive. Everything I need is a gift of the Holy Spirit. I don't need to ask for what's been given already. But I do need to use it. That's when I am utterly amazed at what has been provided. "For all things are yours; whether Paul, or Apollos, or the world, or life, or death, or the present, or the future, all are yours, and you are Christ's and Christ is God's." Paul ticks off the unbelievable resources. When he talks about Paul, Apollos, Cephas—leaders in the early church around whom divisive loyalties foolishly formed—I am reminded of the people who helped me find the adventure in Christ, and all the people who are his love incarnate to me. But that's not all. The world is mine to enjoy. Life is not a drudgery but a never ending succession of God's interventions and infusions of guidance and power. Death is no longer an enemy but an anticipated transition to a fuller life. The present, therefore, can be lived as if it were the only moment I will ever have. Fear of the future is over. I cannot drift out of the sphere of his care. Even the difficulties and tragedies—the worst I or someone else can do—can be used for the best he wants for me. That's living, and I am deeply gratified!

All this is because we belong to Christ. What we observe in his charisma is ours. "These things which I have done, you shall do also . . . and greater things." The great evidence of the presence of the Messiah is the messianic people, extensions of the incarnation in whom all the prophecies of old are being evidenced.

I am convinced that the reason we don't live the life our Lord intended is that we don't believe that indeed all things are ours. We don't know what we've been given. Nor do we know what's available. And we are too arrogantly self-sufficient to admit our need. We are like the farmer who lived in abject poverty without knowing that beneath his barren, dusty, uncultivatable land was a very resourceful oil well. His remark to his wife after the discovery was most telling: "And to think we lived here all these years without knowing how rich we were!"

I can vividly remember one early morning of my first week in Hollywood. I took a walk to the top of Mount Hollywood. From that vantage point I could look over the city of Los Angeles and on out to the Pacific. Below me I could see my church building and imagined my people in the homes, apartments, and offices below. Some were still on the streaming freeway on their way to work. Suddenly, I was gripped by the question, "What do you want to have happen to these people and their church and through it to that needy city? What's their fondest hope?" I reviewed my dream of what the church and contemporary Christians have been called to model for the world. Then I was aware there was someone else there. I felt his strong, gracious, challenging presence. "Are you ready?" he asked. "You need my power to fulfill my dream! Are you willing?"

Then a prayer by William Booth came to mind:

I will tell you the secret: God has had All that there was of me. There have been men with greater brains than I, even with greater opportunities, but from the day I got the poor of London on my heart and caught a vision of what Jesus Christ could do with me and them, on that day I made up my mind that God should have all of William Booth there was. And if there is anything of power in the Salvation Army, it is because God has had all the adoration of my heart, all the power of my will, and all the influence of my life.

It was then that I had to answer, "Lloyd, do I have all that there is of you?"

Do you sense what's happened to us? We have been taken hold of by history's greatest dreamer, eternity's indefatigable visionary. His name is Jesus. He has a dream, a plan, a power for you and me! What he came to do two thousand years ago he picks up again with you and me. Do you hear his drumbeat, will you march to its cadences? He is up to nothing less than the transformation of our lives and through us, all realms of life until the kingdoms of this world become the kingdom of our Lord.

But immediately self-doubt and ambivalence rise to the surface of our minds. Our evading excuses race to fill the gap between what we are and our Lord's dream for us. We need to experience what David Roberts found—"I spent twenty years trying to come to terms with my doubts. Then one day it dawned on me that I had better come to terms with my faith. Now I have passed from the agony of questions I cannot answer into the agony of answers I cannot escape. And it's a great relief!"

It's when we begin to doubt our self-doubts and begin to trust Jesus Christ for his dream and the power to fulfill it that the miracle begins.

Jesus Christ wants to know what we expect. Do we expect what he expects? How much do we want his dream?

He reaches out to each of us right now. He says, "Take my hand, rise up and walk!" Our future and the future of our church hangs in the balance. All excuses are brushed aside. All reservations melt away, and we see only Jesus. "Do you want to be healed? Do you want my dream?" Then we reach out, and he grasps our hand. And suddenly we feel new life in our paralyzed spirits, and we are free to walk with him and run with him and with him serve a paralytic world.

CHAPTER 5

Unrecognized Answers to Prayer

Charisma is given to us through prayer. Yet many Christians who pray do not have charisma. In fact, some have prayed for power and gifts and feel their prayers are unanswered. Is God playing games? Is charisma for some and not for others? Does God have favorites? Or could it be that our problem is in recognizing his answers to our prayers?

If you are like most, you have had some difficulty. Most of us not only have a problem with prayer as a natural, spontaneous conversation with the Lord, but we also have confusion recognizing the answers to prayer once we have prayed. But don't be too hard on yourself. We are in the good company of the early church. These outstanding saints also had difficulties recognizing God's answers to their prayers. The humorous passage in Acts, chapter 12, of how the church prayed for Peter and then did not, or would not, recognize God's answers to their prayers gives us some comfort that these great athletes of the Spirit also had sagging prayer muscles, shortness of breadth, and dimness of vision. This incident crystallizes a general prayer

problem they continually faced in discerning the Lord's
direction in answered prayer. But come along, perhaps we
can learn something from this humorous passage.

The drama in this passage is vivid and appealing. The
inner band of the faithful gathered in their familiar,
memory-filled upper room in John Mark's home in
Jerusalem. This was headquarters for the fellowship. In
these now sacred surroundings they had experienced the
Lord's love in the Last Supper and had heard his
heartrending words of departure. Seated on these same old
cushions they had waited for the promise of the Holy Spirit.
Often they had returned to the room for fresh direction and
vision. And here they were again.

This night they were together in fear and trembling. In
spite of all they had seen and experienced of God's power in
recent days, they sat shivering in fear for their lives. A sick,
solicitous king, Herod Agrippa I, had learned a terrible
thing. He found that his weak relationship with the hostile
Jews he had to rule was strengthened by persecution of the
Christians. The hostility of the Jews to the followers of the
Way grew deeper each day. Herod had experimented with
James, the brother of John. His execution had so pleased
the Jews who hated the Christians that he had arrested the
popular leader of the Christians, Simon Peter himself.

"What would be the most spectacular way of public
execution for this one?" Herod mused.

Until he could discern the most effective execution,
Herod placed him in prison, probably the Tower of Antonia,
with four special guards, one at each side, chained to Peter,
and two at the prison door. No chance of escape now, Herod
thought—and so did the Church, but they prayed for Peter.

Luke closes the opening introduction to the drama with
his often repeated, victorious note of the superceding,
intervening power of the Lord. Using this familiar

confidence-building conjunction, he paints the black, impossible picture and then gives the hint of what the Lord is able to do. "So Peter was kept in prison; *but* earnest prayer for him was made to God by the church" (Acts 12:5).

Can you picture the vivid contrast? Look at it. On the one hand we see the power of Rome focused in a local ruler and his legions appointed by Rome to rule. All of the then known military weight of the Empire could be brought to bear in this little pinpoint of the vast regions of Roman dominion. On the other hand we see a little unarmed band of men and women shaking behind locked doors. They had come together with an odd mixture of consternation and conviction: fear for their very lives, freedom in the knowledge that God was speaking to them even in this.

What would happen to Peter? Who would be arrested next? If they lost Peter, what would happen to the church? With these questions burning in their hearts, they began to pray. First one, and then another; a time of silence; a hymn of praise; and then more prayer for Peter. Seems absurd, doesn't it? What could these insignificant people do against the mighty legions of Rome, the chains about Peter, the guards, an impenetrable prison?

Well, there was little they could *do*. They had to wait—and pray. And here was the profound difference between the Roman Empire and the primitive church: they believed that Jesus was alive, that he was there with them, that prayer was the lifeline of communication with him. Jesus and the power of prayer to him gave hope in a hopeless situation.

Ah, now the plot thickens with humor and pathos. The Lord heard the prayers of the church for Peter and became the unseen mover and manipulator of the destinies of men, according to his will and plan. Peter is awakened in prison by a messenger from the Lord, freed from his chains miraculously without waking the guards, and led out of the prison, first through the prison room door, then past the sentries, and finally through the iron gate leading to the city. Once released, Peter immediately proceeded to the fellowship of the church at John Mark's house. How joyous he must have been with this new evidence of the Lord's intervening love. Unheeding of the danger of arrest, he walked through the streets with the lilt of a man who knows he is the incarnate answer to prayer. Imagine how you would feel if you knew that we were all praying for your healing and you came here personally to show us the healing God had performed. Think of the excitement! Perhaps coming to church each week ought to be like that.

At John Mark's house, Peter knocked at the outside street gate. A maid named Rhoda was delegated to cautiously see who was the interrupter of their prayers. When Peter saw her coming to the gate he called to her a joyous, victorious greeting in the name of the Lord.

Now there follows a bit of drama which is quite unbelievable and very telling. From it we learn a great deal about the prayers of the early church and more than we want to know about human nature.

Rhoda reacts to Peter's greeting with complete emotional befuddlement: "It can't be Peter!" she exclaimed. "Oh my! What shall I do? Praise the Lord! Peter is free! Oh dear, can it be true? What shall I do?" Can't you see her or yourself in the same situation? Instead of opening the gate, welcoming Peter in with a kiss of peace and rejoicing, she scurries and skedaddles to tell the others.

"Why they won't, they can't, believe it!" And she was right. "You have lost your mind, Rhoda! You are out of your senses! Peter could not be here! He's in prison! The Tower of Antonia at that! Think of the guards and the chains! Come off it, Rhoda! You have seen a ghost! Don't make jest with us in this way!"

But then in the midst of the din of the unbelieving chatter something happened and then again, and they all heard it. There was another knock at the gate. They looked at each other. Could it possibly be true? Suppressed hope now began to erupt within them, and they all rushed together to the gate.

And there he was, prisoner set free, beloved leader, rock of the faith, Simon Peter! And they were amazed! Why were they amazed, surprised? Why didn't they immediately fall back into prayer saying,

Thank you, Lord
We've been praying
We know you heard us
Now thank you for your answer
We know this is from you.

Two possible reasons for the surprise are painfully clear. Either they had only prayed general prayers for Peter and had not asked that he be released and so were amazed at how little faith they had and at how much beyond their prayer God had answered. Or they had prayed for Peter's release but did not really believe that it would happen. In either case we see that praying had already become perfunctory and had lost the vitality of belief that the Lord really hears and answers prayer.

Perhaps they had prayed for Peter's instability. Some of the same old problems were still evident and burst out every so often. Suppose they prayed that under pressure he would be the true rock of faith the Lord had declared him to be. If so, then the church was amazed because God answered way beyond their vision to pray.

How like most of us! We receive not because we ask not. Our prayers are meager and subdued because we do not really believe that God will answer according to his timing and will. Ours is to ask with freedom and abandon, His is to determine the advisability of the answer according to his fatherly wisdom and love.

But what if the early church had prayed for release? Could it be that they had prayed for something without really believing that it could be done if according to God's will? Their reactions were rather strong. Remember they told Rhoda she was mad. Others argued with her that it must have been his angel.

Whatever the real situation was, the point of the incident for us is that they prayed and then could not recognize the answer when it came. There seem to be several reasons incarnate in the different types of people in the situation. Perhaps we will find ourselves among them.

First, there were those who could not recognize and appropriate the Lord's answer because of emotional excitement. Rhoda was so excited at seeing Peter that she could not accept the Lord's answer to her prayers in his presence. Know anyone like that? Ever pray so long and hard for something and find that when God answers you are so emotionally unraveled that you can't take advantage of the blessing?

I think of the mother who prayed for her son's safe return for a leave from Vietnam. When he arrived home in answer to her prayer, she was so excited that she could not relax and enjoy him. Instead, she fussed and fumed about how God could let a war like that go on. She spent all of her time cooking sumptuous meals and had no time for the deep conversation the son needed more than the culinary artistry. By the end of the leave the boy was glad to get back to his unit.

A man praying for new opportunities to advance in his work received a new responsibility and position at work. For some reason he did not see the advancement as a natural answer to prayer. The responsibility was great and beyond his human abilities. He should have to depend on God for wisdom and insight. But instead of quiet trust in the same God to whom he had prayed, he got excited and nervous and under the pressure lost the God-given opportunity for tremendous good.

Somewhat the same problem existed with a couple and their child. They had prayed for years about their child's school work. Then, almost overnight, there was an obvious change which continued to improve. The parents could find no logical explanation and reacted with such excitement that it frightened the child back into the frustration causing the problem. They couldn't quietly say, "Thank you, Lord, we knew you would do it, and now we praise you for it. Someday, in your own way, make the source of blessing known to our child."

I often wonder if highly pressured, cause-oriented people don't get so worked up about the cause they are promoting that they are unable to see the answers to prayer the Lord is offering. I met a woman like that this summer. She was terribly steamed up about religion in public education. I appreciated her excitement and shared many of her views about secularization. But when I quietly told her about some of the answers to prayer we were finding through our committed educators, she could not hear me. I told her about advances in our church's lay ministries in education in this matter, but she could not stop her harangue long enough to say, "Well now, isn't that wonderful! I knew God would answer our prayers."

But there were other reasons why the early church found it difficult to accept Peter as an answer to their prayer. Another was unbelief. Some of them could not accept that the thing for which they had prayed actually had happened. How often we miss God's best because we are not able to extend the faith we had to pray, to receive the very thing for which we prayed. Most of us are praying way beyond where we are living. We glibly ask for things we don't believe will ever occur.

Listen to our prayers on Sunday morning! We pray for peace, but how many of us really believe that God can straighten out the ambiguous issues of the power struggle in our world? We ask for startling things for people, with tongue in cheek. We pray for healing and yet expect continued illness and death. Listen in on your own prayers. Do you really believe that what you are praying for could happen? Most of our prayers are resignation.

Prayer is a dangerous but wonderful thing. God does answer every prayer—not always as we had planned or had hoped, but he does answer. This is why the amazement of the early church is such a challenge to us. We pray blissfully on about earthshaking matters but find it difficult to believe when he answers.

But there were others there in the upper room—there were the arguers. Every church has them: people who have a need to be recognized for their point of view. Say anything or do anything, and it should have been said or done some other way. While Peter waited at the gate, they argued about whether it was really Peter or an angel. They could not accept Rhoda's testimony at face value and receive Peter joyfully.

Think of how often we argue with God about the answers he gives to our prayers. We cannot see the answer because it is counter to our preconceptions of what we had expected.

How well I remember the evening I spent with a group of elders in Bethlehem planning for the future of the church I served there. I was at the height of my ministry, in the middle of my tenth year. But somehow I felt out of the process that night, uninvolved and strangely distant. In the midst of gathering dreams for the future, suddenly I was gripped with an undeniable conviction. It was as if the Lord said to me, "Your ministry in Bethlehem is finished!" The thought persisted, blocking any other thought out of my mind. After it became obvious to me that I was being of very little help to those elders, I excused myself and drove home. On the way home I argued with God about all I had left to do there. Was he quite sure? "Lord, you don't understand the plans and dreams I have for this place." Could it be that I was just exhausted or needed a vacation? No, the conviction that my part of the work was finished lingered.

At home I told my wife, Mary Jane, what I had heard. She tried to help me evaluate what happened to me. As we talked I remembered a time some weeks before in a personal retreat in the Poconos Mountains when I had been led to pray, "Lord, I will go where you want me to go, I will do what you want me to do. Give me your strategy for my life." At the time the prayer seemed unusually drastic and decisive. Now I could see why God had planted the prayer he was about to answer. But why was I so reluctant to hear it when it came? The events of my call to Hollywood moved swiftly in the next few months. I am sure, not only of the correctness of that call, but also of the preparation to be open to it.

I wonder if so-called "unanswered" prayer is often simply prayer which has been answered but we did not like the particular answer. Many times the answer is like Moses' burning bush, but we are too set on the way we expected the answer to stop and recognize that we are standing on the holy ground of God's answer.

Many of us have been praying for years about the renewal of the church; but now that the reformation is on in full force we are arguing with God about some of the changes which are taking place in the church's struggle for relevance and authenticity. Others of us have been

screaming long and hard about democracy and praying for
our nation, but now argue with God about the way he is
answering in the difficult challenges. Too fast, Lord! Hold it
up! We're not ready!

But there was another group, not mentioned specifically,
but obviously there, from a study of the context of the
chapters surrounding the passage. There was a group who
were blocked from receiving God's answer because of
personal feelings about the one for whom they prayed.

Even as early as this in Christian history there was
conflict in the early church. The Hebrew Christians held
the line for converts to Christ being introduced into the
Hebrew laws before coming fully into Christ. Others,
however, believed that the gospel was for the Gentiles,
without the requirements of Judaism. The battle raged on,
and this event is sandwiched between Peter's ministry with
Gentile Cornelius and the official review by James, the
brother of Jesus, and the officials of the church.

Feelings ran high among the saints of the church. These
feelings could have caused real feelings of ambivalence
among some of the band there in the upper room. Could it
be that they prayed for Peter and were really blocked about
how God answered. I wonder.

Perhaps the reason some of us cannot recognize God's
answers is that we do not really want the very thing for
which we pray. We know that an answer to prayer will
involve us in a change of our own attitude and relationship.

I remember a woman who prayed for years that her
marriage would become Christian in attitude and fact. She
prayed for her husband's conversion and obedience to
Christ. Then one day what she had asked for was granted,
and he returned home as a new man in Christ. Now her
security of praying for an unbelieving husband and blaming
him for an unchristian marriage was gone. Her shrewish

characteristics which she had never allowed Christ to change were exposed. She really had never wanted the marriage changed at the expense of changing herself.

Or what about the woman who was very concerned about witnessing to others about her faith, and the only answer she got was that a neighbor whom she despised always came over for morning coffee? Peter at a coffee klatch! Peter at the gate! Her situation was very much like a man in a New York suburb who did not like what was going on in his church. The more he prayed about it, the more hostile he felt. He had served as an officer and now seemed put on the shelf. His answer came in instructions to pray another prayer—no solution, just another prayer. He felt compelled to pray, "Lord, I'm the trouble with this church. Start with me." What an answer!

Often the most difficult answers to prayer are those which prescribe some change in ourselves or our cherished way of doing things. Sometimes we actually get what we pray for and sometimes something for which we never bargained.

But Peter kept knocking—praise God for that. He didn't turn on his heel in disgust and hurt. Peter persisted as the God-given answer to their prayer until they recognized and received him. There are many unrecognized answers at the gate knocking. The source of our confidence is expressed by John, Peter's faithful companion who later wrote to the church, "And this is the confidence which we have in him, that if we ask anything according to his will he hears us. And if we know that he hears us in whatever we ask, we know that we have obtained the requests made of him" (I John 5:14-15). Memorize these words, bind them in your being, and repeat them every day and in every situation of need.

Now if this is true, we should live and pray and receive

differently. Perhaps our deepest prayer should be, "Lord, make me a daring prayer. Help me to see the prayers you have already answered. Give me grace to look differently at the people for whom I have prayed. Free me to receive your answers in strange packages and unusual, unexpected circumstances. Lord, give me freedom to recognize your answers to prayer."

What does all this have to say about the question with which we began? Simply this: Charisma is grace-giftedness as we have said previously. Grace has already been given. The gifts of the Spirit are available as equipment for involvement in our Lord's ministry. We should not pray for charisma, but to grow in grace; we should not covet the gifts of God for our aggrandizement, but for effectiveness in our concern for people and our difficult problems.

The scripture we have exposited tells me to relax and to dare to believe that I will have all I need for every moment. If I have faithfully prayed for grace and gifts to mediate it, I will have it.

This has been difficult for me to learn, but it's getting easier all the time. Everything I really need is in God's charismatic gifts—wisdom, knowledge, faith, discernment, miracles, freedom to praise in spite anything or anyone. All that I want to manifest in my relationships is expressed in the fruit of the Spirit—love, joy, peace, patience, kindness, goodness, faithfulness, gentleness, self-control.

But to seek these things or to try to produce them is to fall into a tender trap. They are gifts unavailable without the Giver, fruit inseparable from the vine himself. Seek him and be willing to be amazed; long for him and dare to believe nothing is impossible. Once we have that, all other answers to prayer will be dull by comparison!

CHAPTER 6

Come Alive and Live Forever

"But thanks be to God, who gives us the victory through our Lord Jesus Christ." I Corinthians 15:57

"That I may know him and the power of his resurrection." Philippians 3:10

"Then the other disciple, who reached the tomb first, also went in, and he saw and believed." John 20:8

It had been a long, agonizing night. Sleep would not bless me with a few moments of relief. An immobilizing numbness pervaded my mind and body. Inside I trembled with grief, outside I shook with fear. I hoped that the other disciples seated listlessly about the upper room did not realize. But they were too enveloped in their own pall of remorse to notice or care.

The night noises were interrupted by the dawn sounds of voices and movements on the street below. Would Pilate's soldiers find us? Would some traitor betray us and expose our secret hiding place?

The first rays of dawn pierced through the small opening in the stone and clay wall. Another day—what would this day bring? Discovery, trial, our own crucifixion?

My heart ached with such excruciating disappointment I wished I could die—and was afraid that I wouldn't. I felt like a trapped animal. There was no place to turn, nowhere to go, no pause in the painful loneliness, no relief from the dull throb of discouragement.

I tried not to think about what had happened. But irresistibly my mind darted back to Golgotha and the pitiful picture etched indelibly on my whole being. Oh, how I love Jesus! His words kept tumbling restlessly about in my mind. I could not stop their relentless repetition. "It is finished . . . it is finished . . ."

The dreadful disappointment I had felt standing there desperately clutching his mother's arm now had spiralled down to the deepest pit of my inner feelings. Finished indeed! That's how *I* felt! Finished! It was all over now, I was sure of that, and I too was finished. There was little to do now but secretly anoint and prepare Jesus' body for permanent burial. My mother Salome, Mary Magdalene, and the other women had left long before dawn to do that. I never wanted to dream, hope, live again.

That caused fear to be mingled with guilt. With affection I reached over to the empty pad beside me. It had only been a few hours before when Jesus had celebrated the Passover with us in this very place. I could almost recapture the feeling I had when he said, "Tonight someone will betray me!" We all looked stunned and shocked! It was Peter who had prompted me to ask, "Who is it Lord?"

Was it anger, hatred, or the desire to rip Judas apart when he dipped his hand in the dish? I don't know; all I can remember now is that it all became clear to me in that moment; it was bitterly apparent that what he had tried to tell us would come true. He would be delivered into the hands of evil men, the end was sure.

That's when I collapsed. He had called me John, a son of Thunder, but now the only thunder in me was the crashing waves of a hurricane of horror. I wanted to help him, but I couldn't. I could not keep back the tears; the sobs were irrepressible. I fell on my Master's chest and sobbed like a child. I will never forget the inclusive warmth of those arms as they enfolded me and held me with reassuring love.

Now those arms had been stretched mercilessly on the crossbar and hoisted up on the vertical stake. He twisted and writhed until he died. And with him, something in me, anything of hope or value, died too.

Now my mind darted back impellingly over the three years of unimaginable joy and adventure. I remembered when I first knew our destinies were inextricably intertwined. I had gone to hear John the Baptist at the River Jordan miles from my home. I will never forget the radiance on his face when he came over the hillside toward the river. John paused and looked intently and then shouted words that jarred my soul, "Behold, the Lamb of God!" I should have known then—a man a Lamb of God? What do they do with the Lamb but sacrifice!

And then a few weeks later, he came to the Sea of Galilee where James, my father Zebedee, and I were mending nets beside the sea. The warmth of that moment's memory tempered the present cold chill of my soul. "Come follow me, and I will make you fishers of men!" And follow we did for the three best years of our lives.

But I had given him difficulty at every turn. My fierce competitiveness, my lopsided ego, my temper, my precipitous zeal were always causing him disappointment. Perhaps this was the reason he made me his close and trusted friend. I needed him most of all! Memories of striding across the countryside, sailing on the sea, healing the sick, declaring the kingdom of God all flooded my mind. But each joy was punctuated by stabbing reminders of how often I disappointed him. I constantly stumbled over my inept judgments, impatient arguing, and fiery consternation. I wanted the kingdom, I wanted Jesus to be king, and I wanted to share his earthly power with a passion. I can still remember when I asked to sit on his right hand when he came into power. His look of compassion lingered in my mind. "Are you able to drink the cup that I must drink?" I remember saying that I was able. I sat at his right hand, all right, but it was here, at the Passover, and the announcement of his death. Able? Not at all!

Now the thoughts raced at heightened speed. The denial with Peter in the courtyard, the terrible scourging, the mocking crowd crying "crucify him," the pathetic hours beneath the cross; his tender words to Mary, "Behold your son." He thought about me, cared for me even then!

But that was all over now. There was nothing left to do but wait for a safe moment to escape from Jerusalem, to return to the Sea of Galilee, and pick up the pieces of a shattered dream.

Then suddenly, quick, hurried footsteps on the stone stairs to the upper room broke into my self-pitying mourning. Wild, frenzied, persistently impatient knocking on the tightly bolted door sent terror into my heart.

They've found us! Panic filled the room. The knocking continued. What could we do? Then relief flashed across the disciples' faces. We heard Mary's voice through the timbers of the heavy door. Immediately we lifted the heavy door jam, ominously reminiscent of the cross bar of crucifixion. We opened the door, and the women burst into the room. Their faces were flushed with excitement and joy. They babbled with amazement. Their grief was gone!

"When we got to the Garden," they said, "the stone was rolled away!"

"What are you saying?!" I asked.

"We're trying to tell you that the stone was rolled away!"

"And the body of Jesus?" asked one disciple after another.

"Gone!" they said.

"Gone?" we cried.

"Yes, the tomb was empty, in a way . . ."

Now the women looked at each other, not sure how to explain what they had experienced. Their expression was filled with wonderment and awe.

"The tomb was empty, except . . ."

"Except what?" we urged impatiently.

"Except for the grave clothes . . . they were still there, but Jesus was gone! We found the tomb without difficulty. The sun was just rising. We were wondering if we were strong enough to roll the stone when we entered the garden and to our complete surprise, we saw that it was already rolled back! We were terribly frightened, wondering if someone had tampered with the tomb. We mustered our courage and cautiously entered the tomb. The body of the Lord was not there! But there was a young man dressed in a white robe. We were so frightened we could not speak. But he spoke to us! *Oh, did he speak to us!*"

"What did he say?" we chorused with one voice.

Cautiously, measuring their words, but then overcome with excitement, they blurted out, "He said, 'Do not be amazed. You seek Jesus of Nazareth, who was crucified? He is risen, he is not here; see for yourselves again, the place where they laid him.'"

"Did he say anything else, mother?" I asked. "Think! Did he say anything else?"

Salome beamed with uncontainable pride and affirmation known only to a mother.

"Yes," she said, "he told us to go tell you—the disciples."

That's all I needed to hear! I could not contain myself any longer. I looked at Peter.

"Let's go!" we said in unison.

The two of us shot out of the room like arrows sent from an archer's strong bow. I can still feel the surge of energy which flowed through my body as I ran down the road toward Joseph's Garden.

All fear was abandoned now. I was impatient with my feet; they could not run fast enough. My heart was pounding. What did all this mean? Did someone steal the body? Risen? Risen? How could that be? Peter was ahead of me, running as fast as he could. I overtook him in my breathless urgency and reached the tomb first.

I stood there panting; my heart was racing, my mind spinning wildly. Then suddenly I was afraid. I couldn't go in the tomb! Would he still be there? Were the women just suffering from shock?

Peter reached me at the tomb, but did not stop. He pushed me aside and stumbled compulsively into the tomb. His impetuous courage broke my catatonic spell, and I lunged forward into the tomb. I saw it! Do you hear me, I saw it! The grave clothes were there, but Jesus was gone! I will never forget as long as I live the look Peter and I exchanged. It's true! It's too good to be true, but it's too true to be denied!

We walked out of the tomb,   recklessly grasping each other's arms. We paced back and forth, trying to gather our thoughts.

"What does this mean?" we asked each other. We were too bewildered to know what to say or how to make sense of it.

There was an overwhelming power in that Garden which stirred something which had died within us. I have never heard birds sing so magnificently! The sky was crystal clear and bluer than any ocean. The flowers swayed in the breeze, and the palm, olive, and fig trees almost danced to a majestic rhythm. Something had happened here! We were sure of that! The same feeling we had shared on the Mount of Transfiguration now leaped within us, but now it was infinitely greater. We didn't know whether to kneel or sing or shout.

Then a strange, mysterious, tingling sensation pervaded our bodies. Suddenly my thoughts were filled with the Master's words. It was as if a treasure chest in our memory was opened, and we took out the flashing jewels one by one and examined them with delight. "On the third day I will rise." "I am the resurrection and the life." "Because I live you shall live also!" We have not understood what he meant. Could it now be true? Jesus alive? We walked back thoughtfully to the upper room. How would we tell the others? Would they believe us?

The morning was spent in urgent conversation. But the others would not accept what we had seen. Especially Thomas. Meanwhile Mary went to the tomb again. When she returned, the same good news. She flung open the door, shouting uncontainably with a radiant face and jubilant voice, "I have seen the Lord!"

Joy is the only adequate word I can use to tell you how I felt. Three days without sleep, yet my body felt stronger than ever before. My mind was filled with hope! And within me there sprang a song of gladness that made the whole world alive with expectation.

The day passed with vivid dreams rekindled. We were like unborn babes still in the womb, restless to be born, counting the labor pains of a rebirth of hope.

Then it happened! Jesus came amongst us! He was there, alive, risen, triumphant! He greeted each of us. What a reunion it was! We began to sing, softly at first, then with a gusto which must have been heard in the streets. "He is risen! He is risen indeed!" When we quieted briefly, he spoke to us words we shall never forget. "As the Father has sent me, even so I am sending you."

We all fell on our knees. The room was alive with his power. We all felt it. You can feel it, can't you? Then a strange quickening began in all of us. We felt a new vision and vitality.

"Receive the Holy Spirit! If you forgive anyone's sins, they are forgiven, if you refuse to forgive them they are unforgiven." The same message he had given us before. The kingdom *is* at hand! Jesus is alive!

The stirring account of John's realization of the resurrection helps us to relive what happened that first Easter. I have tried carefully to recapture the mood of the upper room before and after Easter because it helps us to identify with both the abject despair of life without the good news of the resurrection and then to feel the abundant surge of the glorious exhultation after the victory of Christ over death.

Through the eyes of John the Beloved Disciple we have lived, seen, felt that resurrection morning. But that's only the beginning. What happened to John because of the resurrection is the impelling good news for you and me. What occurred as a result can happen to us!

By this time you have discerned that John is my favorite disciple. Why do I love him? Perhaps it is because he is the one whom Jesus loved with the intimate understanding of brother, companion, and friend. Or perhaps it is because I see in him the amazing combination of viable intellect, tender compassion, sensitive emotion, fiery and intense zeal, ardent enthusiasm, and bold courage. But perhaps it's because I see in him most of the problems which we face.

When I live empathetically in his skin, feel what he felt, witness what he saw, experience the transformation he went through, I know there's hope for you and me.

The picture of John there in the upper room after the first encounter with the reality of the resurrection recaptures the mood and plight of most of us. We have seen enough, heard enough to make the fact of the resurrection undeniable, but not enough to have the resurrection happen to us.

I am convinced that John was the same person he had always been as he sat there in the upper room during that first Easter Day. The only difference was that he was disarmed by an alarming, unsettling possibility.

In character, John was no different than he was the day Jesus called him from his nets. History's description of him as the Beloved Disciple is misleading. We have misrepresented this firebrand, often depicting him as a delicate, beardless dreamer. What he later became after the resurrection should not distract us from identification with him on that day when what happened to Jesus happened in him.

Here was a man who matched the sea on which he sailed. He knew tender moments of calm interrupted by tempestuous storms, tornados of anger, swells of impetuous outbursts. Living in the presence of greatness does not make one great! Nor did three years with Jesus change John. To the very end of Jesus' earthly ministry there brewed in John a compound of competitive ambition, jealousy, conceit, self-centered sensitiveness, uncontrollable emotion, and violent temper.

That's good news for you and me! In a sense, our acquaintance with Jesus was like John's life before the resurrection got hold of him. We know what Jesus said; we have rehearsed what that should mean to us; we have longed to be different; but we simply are the same old

personalities we ever were. Often we have thought that if
we could have sat at the Mount of Beatitude and heard the
Sermon on the Mount, felt his touch of healing, caught his
impelling vision for the kingdom, we could live this
Christian life with faithfulness. Not so!

Like John on that Easter Day, we have a hope without
help, a dream without dynamism, teaching without transformation, explanation without exhilaration. Along with our
nation we are brokenhearted by human failure, disil-
lusioned with our own inadequacies, nervous over the
tensions of life, frightened by the future. Like John, we
have learned all we need of the facts. We have tried to love
and have ended up in distorted self-pity. We have tried to
help others and have met our own needs in a defeating
countertransference.

Last Easter, I met a woman in the parking lot on her way
to early worship. I greeted her joyously. She did not share
my mood. Grief like a ploughman had furrowed her brow.
Six months before she had lost her husband in a tragic
death, leaving her to raise four children. In desperation, she
had become a Christian and tried to order her home around
the teachings and example of the Savior. But no success
story, this! The children's grief flowed in rebellion against
her. Finances were a persistent problem. Working all day
and struggling with housework until late in the evening left
her exhausted.

"How's it going?" I asked.

"I'm not sure how long I can hang on!" she said
desperately and turned away holding back the tears. She
had everything the Christian faith offered, except the lifting
power to live it!

I talked to a man the other day over lunch. His world had
just collapsed with the discovery that his wife had had an
affair with his closest friend. She has asked for forgiveness,

a chance to begin again. I'll never forget the look on this
man's face. He has been a Christian since childhood, in the
church as long as he can remember, a part of a men's Bible
study group for years. His voice quivered when he said,
"With all that I have heard about forgiveness and
supposedly experienced for myself, I can't forgive my wife!
I can't give myself to her or accept her back with trust.
Where can I find the power to do that? It's just not in me!"
Can Easter make a difference for this man?

A young man on a college campus met me after a speech.
We talked late into the night. "What's so different about
Christianity? I see Christians living like anyone else,
causing the same kind of society as unbelievers, doing the
same loveless, drab thing everyone else is doing. You're
talking about something different—powerful, invigorating,
nonreligious, exciting. How do I find that and still not
become dull and boring like most church members I
know?"

A scientist looked intently across my desk. "Listen, my
child is dying; don't give me platitudes, I need something to
give me courage. I'm an intellectual. Words are cheap with
me, and theories are my stock and trade. Help me! I love
her so!" Can the empty tomb give this man hope?

A bright young director caught my arm as I was leaving a
broadcast studio recently. "Have you got a minute?" he
asked and walked with me to my car. "I've got a fantastic
future. All the things I ever wanted to do, I am doing all at
once. It's exciting. But when I am alone in my apartment
late at night, I begin to wonder about where it's all going.
My gal wants more than intimacy without entangling
alliances, you know what I mean. I realize that I am
'thinging-it' with her, but I am afraid of all that responsibility. With my career and all, I guess I don't know what I
want. Are you going to say anything this Easter for

swinging singles like me who are swinging into nothing-
ness?" Can the Risen Christ do anything for this man?

A young high school student intently sits within my eye
range every Sunday morning. He is one of the most avid
listeners I have ever had. I found him waiting outside my
office one Sunday after church. His bright countenance,
easy manner, and up-to-date style communicated potential
and sharpness. "I am with you all the way on Sunday
morning. But it's during the week at school, on dates, and
on the soccer field that it just doesn't work for me. You'd
probably never guess it, but inside I'm terribly insecure and
frightened. People tell me I'll get over that when I grow up,
but I'm not so sure; the people who say this to me are forty,
and they are still insecure and frightened—and they say
they're Christians! I don't want to listen to you anymore
unless the power I feel here on Sunday can get inside me
where I need it!" Can the power of the resurrection help a
teenager?

A retired couple in their late sixties confessed that they
had worked all their lives to relax and enjoy themselves. We
sat together in their beautiful, affluent home. "All we know
how to do is work hard. We've got all the money we need to
have fun, only we don't know how. How do you stop trying
to get ahead when you're already ahead?" Is it ever too late
to join the adventure of the Easter people?

A lovely widow in her late fifties left church alone. She
pressed my hand warmly. "It was great this morning, but
have you ever had Sunday dinner alone? That's the hardest
time of the week." Can the living Christ do anything about
loneliness?

A man with a sexual division in his character tried to
convince me that his way of life was God-ordained and not
the result of psychological and family dynamics. I listened
carefully. At the end of the monologue he said, "I guess I

just want your sanction. But even if you gave it to me, I'd still have a problem. It's just that there is no permanence, only one relationship after another; who cares about me, for me, as I really am as a person? I am a Christian, but it doesn't seem to make any difference." Can the Lord of life heal our personalities?

So it goes. The Easter parade is filled with people like those I have mentioned. And so many more—the man who has banked the fires of love for the long cold night of endurance in a marriage which is no longer exciting; a woman who worries over her children's success and can't let them go; a family which lost its mother a week ago; a weary business man who is racked with anxiety over his investments; a young couple struggling to love in the language which will fulfill and satisfy each other; an uptight churchman who cannot express affection to his wife and children; a politician who is afraid that Watergate investigations will flow into his office; a lovely writer with style but no story.

But that's not all. There are others in our celebration of new life. They are here because of custom, a faithless familiarity. They are satisfied with things as they are. As a matter of fact, they hope Easter will not be too penetrating, too personal. The insulation is barricaded around their egos, and they hope we can fluff up the surface of festivity, without going too deeply. "Tell us about Jesus, dramatize the resurrection and leave it there in Jerusalem!" they say.

And intermingled in the crowd are the happy people. They can't understand why other people have so many problems. They want to be patient but often get perturbed when things are painted so desperately. The problems of life have never excavated the depths of their souls, and they find the doom and gloom very perturbing if not boring. Life's not that way for them. Easter's no big thing to a

happy person. Oh yes, it's good to have confirmation of their
happiness in the delightful Eastertide and family gather-
ings, but what's all the shouting about? But for these
participants in the Easter parade, there seems to be a gift
for the people who seem to have everything. The good can
be replaced with the best, adjustment with adventure,
self-satisfaction with self-realization, happiness with joy
which shallow happiness, dependent on circumstances,
could never provide.

This applies to us all—the holy but hopeless, the religious
but unreleased, the broken but unhealed, the lovely but
unloved, the self-sufficient but unsatisfied, the beautiful
but unblessed. And the question is: Can it happen again?
Can the resurrection do anything in us, for us, to us,
through us? John would answer a thundering yes which
would roll through the ages to the present.

After the resurrection we see a new John in the
Scriptures and recorded history. What life with Jesus could
never do, the power of the resurrection did in him. The
months that followed that Easter day produced a transformation in his character, motives, relationships, and effectiveness. During the three years with Jesus of Nazareth, he
was merely potential. His passion, verve, creativity, and
energy were all distorted and misdirected. Then Jesus'
resurrection gave him new hope. He appeared repeatedly to
John and the disciples to galvanize the realization that he
was truly alive! The whole world must know that death was
defeated, sin vanquished, and eternity opened. He told him
to wait until he received power. Then fifty days after
Passover, back in that same upper room, Jesus returned in
the power of the Holy Spirit and entered into him to enable
him to live the life Jesus had lived, to change his
squandered dynamism into creative love, and to make him
an example of resurrection living.

There are several dimensions to John's resurrection experience. One was the cross—his old boisterous, impatient, self-centered nature was broken open by that. He had known that Jesus loved him, but the cross sealed it. After the resurrection he looked back and realized what had happened there on Calvary. Jesus died for John! The second dimension was Jesus' resurrection. This liberated John to believe that God could have the ultimate victory in anything! What courage, daring, and boldness that gave him! The third dimension was the experience of Pentecost when the living Christ came to make his home in John's heart. From within, Jesus marshalled John's emotions to love, fired his intellect to speak and write as no fisherman of Galilee had ever written or spoken. History has called him the Christian Plato. The fourth dimension was in living daily with problems, persecution, and pain, totally dependent on the intervening and interpretive power of the living Christ. John became a leader of the resurrection people who moved out into the Palestinian and Asiatic world. We are startled by the liberated John we see after Resurrection and Pentecost. He is a totally different man! He became noted for his love in spite of the difficulties and discouragements the church faced. The Risen Lord captured the electricity in his nature and used it to light the world. Every time we find him in Acts, he is meditating the gracious spirit of love of his Master and Lord. He became a reconciler and healer of relationships, the strategist of the church as the beloved community, and the most contagious lover of persons. The only explanation of this beautiful person is the resurrection. Vitriolic, sour, condemnatory judgmentalism was replaced with sweet, remedial love.

To live with John through those years between the resurrection and his death at old age is to see the Risen Lord in a human personality. Overreaching ambition for himself became passion for people; explosive temper became the driving power to build up people; an intolerant heart was broken open with inclusive affirmation for the least, the lost, and the lonely. Christ can do that for any person who realizes the resurrection.

Even when John was banished by Domitian to Patmos to live in solitude and servitude, he was open to the power of the resurrection. His writings to the early church, written in esoteric apocalyptic language, now stand as the last book in the New Testament. Christ's finished triumph is its constant theme. "Hallelujah! For the Lord God omnipotent reigneth!" His letters to the early church are filled with the theme of love. But the resurrection power was behind it all. Listen to his own testimony.

> Christ was alive when the world began, yet I myself have seen him with my own eyes and listened to him speak. I have touched him with my own hands. He is God's message of Life, This one who is life from God has been shown to us and we guarantee that we have seen him; I am speaking of Christ, who is eternal life. He was with the Father and then shown to us (I John 1:1-2, The Living Bible).

Now feel the pulse beat of Christ's love flaming from John: "Again I say, we are telling you about what we have actually seen and heard, so that you may share the fellowship and the joys we have with the Father and with Jesus Christ his Son"(I John 1:3, The Living Bible). Where does all this lead? Listen to him again. "Dear friends, let us practice loving each other . . . God showed us how much he loved us by sending his only Son . . . since God loved us as much as that, we surely ought to love each other too" (I John 4:7-11, The Living Bible).

Then look at the fourth Gospel. It is John's settled, ripened, seasoned analysis and account of what God did in and for the world in Jesus Christ, his death and resurrection. He could write the majestic words, "For God so loved the world, that He gave his only son that those who believe in him might not perish but have eternal life" because he had been a witness to, a recipient of, and a communicator for, the resurrection. The words stand forever . . . "Then I went too, and saw, and believed [that he had risen]" (John 20:8, The Living Bible).

Until the resurrection is personal it cannot be powerful. John and Paul alike witness to that. At the end of his life Paul uttered his final prayer: "All I want to know is Christ and the power of his resurrection" (Philippians 3:10).

We can never be satisfied with the truth unless we know its power. We cannot get hold of the reality of the resurrection until we allow it to get hold of us. When it is in the first person singular, three things are possible.

1. A realized potential of eternity. I am not talking about the mere endlessness of immortality. That's not the new power Jesus revealed in his resurrection. He said, "I am the resurrection and the life." The two must always be kept together. What God joins together let no man put asunder! When Paul mounts to the crescendo of his dissertation on the resurrection in I Corinthians 15, he confronts the two enemies of life: sin and death. Sin is simply separation from God and life as he meant it to be. The cross ended the power of sin to rob us of the joy of truly abundant living. Death was defeated and no longer has power over us. When we are alive in relationship with Christ, fear of death is ended, anxiety over the grave is gone. We are not only alive forever, we are truly alive right now. Do you believe that? Will your death simply be a transition in living? Eternal life is a quality of life now that death can never end. It's for us right now. But that's dependent on the second gift.

2. The power of the resurrection is a realized power of

personal regeneration. Resurrection spells regeneration. Here again, two things must always be kept together: the new world and the new man. Resurrection is not a passport to heaven, but a power to change us now. It is a present gift, not a wistful longing. Paul says that he wants to know Christ and the power of his resurrection. The two are the same. To know Christ today is to come under the influence of the same power that raised him from the dead. All life is meant to be an Eastertide full of perpetual renewal. Christ's mission is to change us and make us like himself. What a cruel thing an example is without the power to live it. Christ is the best of all examples, but more than that, he can come within us and give us his own Spirit to fulfill the example. The result is that we actually become like him, we are able to do the things he did, and most of all, we are able to love as he loved. The resurrection is the right angle where all the disillusionment, discouragement, and disappointment with life, people, and ourselves is met with power to change us and give us a new beginning. That leads us to the third promise of the power of the resurrection.

3. It is the realized presence of the victorious Savior. Once again two unseparables: our problems and his presence. The purpose of Easter is not to tell us we should live better lives. It is not a time for moralizing or compulsive improvement programs. Easter is the celebration of victory, Christ's and ours. So often we come to church to get insight, wisdom, strength for our preconceived direction. We usually leave disappointed and unchanged. It's because we want his guidance or sanction on our lives to be more religious. That's not Easter. The resurrection happens when men can do nothing for themselves or for God. It is when our knowledge of Jesus' life and message have driven us to cry out, "Lord, I can't do it, I can't change, I can't love, I can't forgive, I can't take it any longer!"

That's when it happens. Only then can we hear him say, "Because I live, you shall live also!" Then we can join the magnificent procession of the Christ-encountered, Christ-liberated, Christ-healed, Christ-changed, Christ-filled people who shout the Easter refrain:

"Thanks be to God who gives us the victory
through Jesus Christ our Lord!"

Have you ever met him? Or having met him, have you ever felt his presence near? Or having felt his presence, have you ever experienced His resurrection lifting you up to the person He created you to be? And having experienced his resurrection, have you ever invited him to make his postresurrection home in you? He is here for you!

We have been in and out of the upper room this morning. Which one is like your heart? When did you identify with John? In the dawning hours after a sleepless, restless night or at evening when Christ appeared and released joy and triumph? Most of us find we are in constant transit between the two. We know Christ is alive but we are still locked in problems and life's impossibilities. Then come to the upper room at Pentecost and experience the living Christ not around, above, beside, but within you!

CHAPTER 7

Where There's Hope There's Life

"Blessed be the God and Father of our Lord Jesus Christ! By his great mercy we have been born anew to a living hope through the resurrection of Jesus Christ from the dead. . . . In this you rejoice."—I Peter 1:3, 6

I have a good friend who is a physician. He has a saying which he repeats as he leaves a patient in a hospital room. After he has checked the charts on the patient's progress, takes his pulse, and discusses his condition, and just before he turns to go, he says, "Well, where there's life, there's hope!"

What I want to say is in bold contradiction to that ambiguous prognosis. In fact, my thesis is just the opposite. I believe that where there's hope, there's life. Hope enables a quality of life; it sets a man free to dare, gives him confidence for daily frustrations, and courage to live adventurously and die courageously. Jesus said, "I came that you might have life abundant." Hope is the key which opens the flood gates of his power and unlocks the flow of his amazing unlimited possibilities.

A group of college students drove their Volkswagen into a filling station. They had beautiful flower decals decoratively arranged all over the car. The gas station attendant asked a very penetrating question. "Do you want me to water the flowers or fill the tank?" That's my question, too. It is because I sense your authentic search for life that I want to do something more than water the decals. To fill the emptiness, I want to talk about the deepest longing in all of our lives: the need for hope. Emil Brunner was right: What oxygen is to the lungs, hope is to the soul.

If you and I could talk personally, as if there were only two of us, I would want to ask you three questions which demand an answer which is intellectually reasonable, personally realizable, and socially responsible. Do you have hope? Is your hope based on a source which is ultimately reliable? Are you a hopeful person who can infuse hope in others? Then, if we could experience the gift of dialogue, I would want to share with you my own search for hope. If I were honest with you, I would tell you of my own excruciating disappointment in trying to find hope in religion, in social structures, in people, and in the futility of futurity. At that point, if I felt the mutual affirmation of fellow strugglers, I would open my inner heart and tell you how hope happened to me.

I realize that I have just stated my profoundest desire for what our time together could mean to us. It is based on an assumption and an assurance. I suggest that we all want to find a lasting hope, and all of us want to be hopeful people. I have sought too long for authentic hope to mock your honest search with presumptuous piety, jaded jargon, or easy equivocation. We are all cut from the same cloth when it comes to wardrobing the future. I don't want to be like the young man in the cartoon proposing to a teenage girl. Her response was, "It will never work, Stephen; you're cola, and

I am uncola." I am assured that beneath the surface we are soul brothers and sisters wanting to find life as it was meant to be: full, exciting, abundant, satisfying, and fulfilling.

I had a theological professor at the University of Edinburgh who said: "The trouble with you Americans is that you get a good idea, jack it up, and put a biblical text under it!" The passage from I Peter is the foundation of everything I want to say. Søren Kierkegaard said that an intellectually honest person must live with a newspaper in one hand and a Bible in the other. One is the tabulation of our hopelessness and the other the source of our hope. When we take what Peter said about hope in one hand and the account of our contemporary confusion in the other, we have a realistic, two-fisted approach to where we are today and what is the only assurance of sanity.

The context tells us what hope is not. The text itself tells us what true hope is. Peter wrote to the early Christians in dispersion, scattered believers out in the Palestinian and Mediterranean world. They had been deprived of all the securities of Jerusalem, separated from the heartbeat of the apostolic fellowship, and forced to live out their faith in a pagan, hostile world. He called them "holy" people, that is, people who belong to God. They had been set apart, called to live in very difficult circumstances with their hope in God and not in Pontus, Galatia, Cappadocia, Asia, or Bithynia. For them Peter focused a triumphant truth which has become the basis of our understanding of hope. "Let us give thanks to the God and Father of our Lord Jesus Christ! Because of his great mercy, he gave us new life by raising Jesus Christ from the dead. This fills us with a living hope."

Context and text blend together for us. We, too, must know what hope is not before we can hear a clear word on what true hope is for us.

First of all, hope is not environmental. Our age is one of

hopelessness. The virulent poison flows in our nation's blood stream. The result is a deepening feeling of emotional unease, of disorientation, of things not working, of wrong decisions made and right ones missed, a profound feeling of things out of sync. The future has invaded the present, and we have been robbed of our anticipation that things will eventually work out. We are left with a visceral feeling of life out of control: the escalation of misunderstood change that won't slow down, the rising distrust of all authority, the breakdown of faith in our institutions, the sickening feeling of futility jarred by the clashing voices and endless complexity, and the lingering inner discontent which has spread like a poison gas across our nation. But the most alarming manifestation of the hopelessness of our time is the sense of futility that we are experiencing. We feel like pathetic numbers caught in the web of technological systems beyond our control.

Everything in life is on some computer card somewhere. Try to straighten out a computerized bill which you have either underpaid or overpaid! The students at UCLA call the computer which holds the memory data about their academic achievement by the name of "Hal." When they want to know how they have done in a course or how many credits they need to graduate, they go and pay for a few moments for Hal to flash up their record on an impersonal screen. A young man went to his professor about his grade. The response was, "How should I know how you did? Go see Hal!"

When this illusion of powerlessness has given illegitimate birth to the idea that if we cannot govern our own lives, then everything is permissible because nothing makes any difference.

Erich Fromm said, "In the nineteenth Century the problem was that 'God is dead'; in the twentieth Century the problem is that man is dead!" The death of our gods has caused the demise of our inadequate hopes. Our hopelessness is a direct result. Fromm was near the truth, but let me reword the implication: The death of or gods has caused the death of man. We have been infected by the terrible virus of syncretism, the worship of many diminutive gods blended together for security. The Lord God is but one of many gods which fortify us against despair. There's a great difference between genuine and common hope. The diminutive, utilitarian gods of our own making and faking are always a means to our ends. They will always disappoint us. This is the cause of our hopelessness today.

In the past decade our cultural gods have been exposed for their inadequacy. The gods of human progress, inventive genius, the future, armed power, financial security, governmental effectiveness, movements to bring human rights and dignity, great leaders, political parties, and urban renewal have fallen from their thrones. They are all unreliable sources of hope. To hope in any of these is to know disappointment and utlimately experience despair.

Our period has been a litmus test for most of us. We have experienced excruciating disappointment in our false hopes of institutions. Because our ultimate security has been mingled with the success of our secondary loyalties of religion, patriotism, leaders, denominational structures, and our cultural patterns, we have suffered deeply as each of these has been tried and found inadequate. We now want God among other gods to save and sustain our culture.

Also, hope is not circumstantial. Our hopelessness today is profoundly personal. We have erected our loved ones, our families and friends, our jobs, our money, and our images to the status of worshipable deities. What we have been or long to become are the driving motives of our lives. There is no greater mercy that the Lord God can show than to lead

us to the desperate end of trusting people and circumstances to bring meaning to our lives. God's people
have always been strangers to culture. Any church or
Christian married to culture or the past or some wish or
dream will be a widow to the future.

Further, hope is not evolved. It does not come as a result
of developmental growth. We do not work up to or into
hope. Most of us look for hope around the next corner. If we
get things worked out or achieve our goals, we expect to
become more hopeful people. Paul was right (Romans
8:24): "For in this hope we are saved. Now hope which is
seen is not hope. For who hopes for what he sees?" Hope is
not the result of the rearrangement of our estrangement.

Yet without hope something dies within us. What we
hope for determines the vitality of our lives. But the
question is: When we have arrived at where we are going,
where will we be; when we get what we want, what will we
have; when we achieve our goals, what will we have
accomplished? Those brinksman-like questions lead us to
the raw edge of hopeless despair. The flights of the human
mind are not from pleasure to pleasure, but from one hope
to another. The past may have fashioned our psyches, but it
is hope which drives us on more than the pleasure of the
past; it is the pull of the future which gives us power to
achieve. The undiscovered, unexperienced, unresolved,
unexplained, untamed pulls us on to the next challenge,
the next adventure, the next day! The battle hymns of hope
set men marching; searching, trying, enduring. Therefore,
there is no sickness which is worse than the hopelessness
which comes from an inadequate source of our hope.

Lastly, hope is not iatrogenic; it is not self-induced. It
does no good to say self-incriminatingly, "I ought to be more
hopeful! What's the matter with me? With all I have and all
the great things which have happened to me, I ought to be

more hopeful!" That doesn't work. Trying harder, thinking more deeply, straining more energetically will not produce more hopefulness. Paul's word to the Corinthians cuts like a razor: "If for this life only we have hope in Christ, we are of all men most to be pitied" (I Corinthians 15:19).

Now we are ready to hear what Peter has to say about what really is the only source of our hope. The first thing he tells us is that hope is inadvertent; it comes from something or someone else. It grows out of the fertile soil of confidence and conviction which no person, place, position, power, or passion will provide. Peter tells us clearly that we have living hope through the resurrection. In I Peter 1:21 the message even becomes clearer, "Through him you have confidence in God, who raised him from the dead and gave him glory, so that your faith and hope are in God."

There it is! Do you feel it? The resurrection breaks the seal of our hopelessness and gives us a dynamic expectation. True hope is always inadvertent, a result of the power of the resurrection.

Let's put it this way. You and I need to know that God is able. We need what he did in Christ not only for an interpretation of the meaning of life but also for an intervention into the futility of life. The question we must answer is: If God could perform the miracles of Easter, can he not pull us out of the doldrums of our diminished dreams? If he could take an ignominious sign of excruciating execution and make it the symbol of exhilarating expectation, can he not deal with our problems? The only satisfactory fulfillment of our emptiness is an empty tomb! God raised Jesus, and that's the only adequate basis of hope for you and me. He was not done when men did their worst at the crucifixion. He did his best and spoke the final word of victory. There is, therefore, no situation, circumstance, or problem which is too big for him.

Indeed! The only sure basis of hope is in the Creator and Lord of Life. It was God himself who came to us in Christ. It was not just a revelation about God or a manifestation of his glory, essence, or essential truth. Christ did not come to convince us of the love of God, but to be with us as the loving God forever and ever. He came not just to preach the living God but to be God over life. And that's why death could not hold him. The life he lived was so filled with the life and power of God that the resurrection followed as naturally as day follows night.

In that context we can say, "What's the worst that could happen to me, that God could not resurrect for his glory?" No wonder Paul could marshall up the worst enemies of life and parade them before his readers as impotent, depleated, and exposed. Life, death, angels, principalities and powers, things to come—all defeated. None can separate us from the love of God.

What more needs to be said? Much more! For many of us have known and believed the hope of the resurrection and often are still hopeless when life tumbles in on us.

Hope is not only inadvertent, it is imputed and infused. It is a gift. That leads us to a further question, and in its answer we find immediate, contemporary, now-oriented hope. Have we ever experienced the resurrection in our own lives? That's just what Peter means by a "living" hope. He says that we are born anew to a living hope. The terms "born anew" and "living hope" are galvanized together.

The resurrection as the basis of our hope must become a personal reality. This happens when we are born anew. Jesus made the reality of this known to Nicodemus. I believe that we experience this once and for all and again and again for all. The new life in Christ is ushered in with a new beginning. We come to that place where we are convinced of our need. We need forgiveness, acceptance, and love. These needs soften, melt, and open us to realize our inadequacies. We know that we are empty, lonely, fearful, and anxious. In response to his love, we commit and surrender the control of our lives to our Lord. Through this we begin a relationship with him. Zinzendorf said, "I have a great need for Christ; I have a great Christ for my need."

But that's only the beginning. Through this experience we know that we are alive forever, that God will never let us go, and that his power is available to us. But we believe only what we continually rediscover. The living hope comes when we personally experience the resurrection in our daily disturbances, discouragements, and despairs. We are born anew to a living hope each time we are brought to the end of our own resources and, after trying everything and everyone else, we turn desperately to our loving Lord who has been waiting for us all along. When the problems or the potentials which face us become insurmountable, we are ready for a fresh experience of the resurrection. Paul said: "We were buried therefore with him by baptism into death, so that as Christ was raised from the dead by the glory of the Father, we too might walk in newness of life" (Romans 6:4). And in another place he said that he died daily. Put these two together and you have the formula for victorious and charismatic living.

In every problem, every relationship, every challenge, there is the decisive moment when we must die that Christ might live within us and the particular circumstance. I have had to learn this again and again in my life. When I first gave my life to Christ, that meant a surrender of my own plans and selfish purposes. But that was only the start. Christ, who was my Savior, now had to become my Lord. In my marriage, my ministry, my plans and programs, there is always that dreadful moment when I must answer the question of who's in charge.

I can remember the time in my marriage when I was forced to realize that I could not love unselfishly and creatively. I can still picture the walk I took out behind my home in Gurnee, Illinois. I stood beside an old pump which had not pumped water for years. And suddenly I felt that my life was like that waterless well. I could not provide the love my wife or the people around me needed. I still can feel the excruciating pain of death to myself which brought me to cry out, "God help me!" And he did. I was born anew to a living hope that God could change me and gave me what has become a truly enriching marriage.

In each of the churches I have served there has been that crucial moment when I had to surrender my voracious hunger for success and popularity and trust my ministry to our Lord. I can mark the decisive change in each of those ministries from those moments. Resurrection to a new level of power and productivity has always resulted.

An old friend of mine who began a new pastorate recently expressed these same discoveries in a letter. "In November and December I 'crashed.' The weight of leaving my old church, the stimulus of the new, very positive response, all took energy in amounts I did not realize. When the excitement was over and we settled down to the nitty-gritty of normal problems, frustrations, and delays, in spite of the good things that were happening and because of the fatigue, I 'lost it in the turn.' My prayers had been prosaic and undisciplined; my study of the Word had been spotty if at all; times for physical exercise and family renewal were too thin. The result of the whole package was depression and a loss of creative motivation that scared the daylights out of me. For a week or ten days I had visions of the shortest pastorate in history; I just did not have the gumption for the necessary disciplines of the office and sermon preparation, and I wondered if really this was the end of this type of ministry. I took a couple of days off during the holidays and spent a lot of time in prayer and rest; the upshot is that I see that, indeed, I am a 'branch' and Christ is the 'vine.' I'm not going to make it without him and his Word. In spite of the 'down,' God kept working. The need for clear priorities, walking the edge of God's will in the midst of excessive demands and slim resources, becomes very important."

I know this to be true of my family. I am a forceful, determined father with images and dreams for my children to fulfill. Each time I let go and trust their future to God, new life floods in. The amazing thing is that I always realize that my expectations were insignificant by comparison to the vision which God had for the people I love.

The same is true for the movements in the church and society which I have fathered and brothered through the years. In each case, my hope was misplaced in the movement itself and eventually was brought to the place of trusting God to bring his resurrection power to lift us to possibilities I had never dreamed would be possible.

There is nothing so depleting as our efforts to work for God. If we hang onto yesterday's worries, tomorrow's fears, and today's anxieties, we will overload and blow the circuits. We were never created to work for God; we were created for God to work through us. Death to self opens the channel. Resurrection makes possible what we could never have done by ourselves.

We will never be without two persistent realities as we live in Christ. We will always have problems—that's life—but we will always have the power of the resurrection—that's hope.

Now, what about you? If you were to share with me as I have with you, what would you say is the thing or relationship in your life where you most need to know God's three invincible "I's"—interpretation, intervention, and infusion? What's aching in you? Who's the source of your frustration? What is it that festers and causes pain?

Do you dare to believe that our Lord has helped you focus that need because right now he is ready to help you to understand, is waiting to invade, is able to give vision and power through his indwelling Spirit. He will not force himself or his salvation upon us. He will wait until we let go of it, commit it to him, turn it over to his guidance, open ourselves to his direction. There are times when we feel we know what we are to do but have no power. We have a rudder but no sail, or the fires are out and we must hammer the cold iron of life's problems.

I talked to a man over lunch last week. He had just been told that his wife had cancer. He was racked with grief. Why did we lunch that day on the heels of this formidable news? The date had been set two months before. Why that day? The Lord did not send the cancer, but he did send me to that man. He had been a Christian for years, is one of Los Angeles' outstanding leaders, and had enjoyed a very happy marriage. Now his whole life seemed to be a *cul de sac* of no exit. After lunch we walked across the street to his office. The grief was boiling beneath the surface, bursting forth out of his eyes and furrowed brow. We closed the door of his office and prayed together for healing, strength, and enabling love. He accepted again the reality of the resurrection—death could not end his wife. Then we prayed for healing; cancer was not too great for God if he willed. But most important of all, I saw a man resurrected from anguish and torturous worry in the middle of an office! Where there's hope there's life!

A few weeks ago I was facing a problem of inadequate funds for a strategic program I felt God had led me to do. The night before the day on which the funds were needed, I was restless most of the night. About four in the morning the Lord said, "Lloyd, give me that problem and go to sleep."

The next day I had an appointment with a man whose time with me had been changed four times because of schedule conflicts. He began our visit in a very unusual way. He told me story after story of incidents when God had intervened in his life to resurrect impossible problems. "This was exactly what I needed to hear," I told him. He asked why. Suddenly, he was counseling me to whom he had come for insight. I told him about my restless night and what I needed for what seemed to be a Spirit-guided program. "Where do you want me to send the check" was his immediate response. As he left the office I was amazed at two things: God's timing—what if that appointment had been one month earlier—and God's provision—why do I worry about the faithfulness of our Lord to provide the resources for what he has willed?

There is a mysterious secret at the core of what I have been saying. It is this. God loves us so much, he wants to be our friend. He is for us and the things in our lives he has willed. Our problem is that after we begin the Christian life we want to live it on our own power. That's the reason he withholds aspects of his blessings until we pray. Praying is not to convince God of what we need, but to grasp what he has and will make available. True prayer is to open ourselves so completely to him that we know how to ask for the things he has willed. There is no lack of power and wisdom to do the things he has guided. There is little communication with him if we pray only for those things we could do on the energy and with the wisdom he has given already. Our prayers are not bold enough because we have not been broken in our aggressive self-assertiveness and trusted him completely.

We are called to be charismatic communicators of this hope. The great need in our day is communicating to a hopeless, non-Christian society, a culture in which the sources of man's hoping are depleted, and a world which has heard the false hopes of religion and is no longer impressed. A world that will only listen again if a bold, contagious apostolate of hope can incarnate hope which has survived the heat of the fire. I find people very ready to hear about a hope like that.

We are supposed to be liberating people of hope whose lives are laboratories of God's Spirit. Then if we will dare to care enough to share what God is doing with the hopelessness of our own lives, we will be able to lead people to that decisive moment of brokenness, trust, and a new beginning. Then we can stand with them and rejoice as the complicated problems unravel. Our contagion will be caught and spread abroad.

But a further question remains, begging attention. Does this quality of hope make any difference in the way we live our daily lives and grapple with the frustrating problems of our age? That question forces me to think of the truly hopeful people I know. Most of them have passed through a difficult period of the exposure of their false hopes. They are people who are free of ultimate allegiance to culture, institutionalized religion, human loyalties which compete with our Lord, and wish-dreams for results in their projects. Status, social approval, and financial security have been faced and seen for what they are: limited hopes. The reason we tolerate injustice in our society or manipulative devices in our relationships is because we are frightened. Our needs are greater than our hope. Moltmann was right, "Hope is nothing more than the expectation of those things which by faith we believed to have been truly promised by God. Those who hope in Christ can no longer put up with reality as it is, but begin to suffer under it, to contradict it. Peace with God means conflict with the world, for the goods

of the promised future stab inexorably into the flesh of any
unfulfilled present."

I enjoy people whose hope in Christ has released them.
These are the people whose decisions I trust, whose advice
I seek, whose companionship I cherish. They are not
always equivocating, reacting defensively. There's no
secondary loyalty which clouds the issues. Not even the
programs we plan together become a hope. Only the
absolute dependence that if anything of value is to be done,
God must do it. Our only task is to discover what he's doing,
where he's breaking through and join and follow him.

When Deborah Kerr was filming *Quo Vadis,* she was
asked by a newspaper reporter if she ever feared the lions.
"No," she replied, "I have read the end of the script!" And so
have we!

The undeniable evidence of the inner experience of hope
in the early Christians was boldness. The Greek word is
parresias, which means freedom of speech, confidence,
and forthrightness. The early Christians lived life in the
imperative mood under the prompting of the Holy Spirit.
Jim Elliot, who was martyred in South America said, "He is
no fool who gives what he cannot keep to gain what he
cannot lose." Peter Drucer has put it directly: "There are
four risks in life: the risk we must accept; the risk we can
afford; the risk we cannot afford to take; the risk we cannot
afford not to take."

Recently I preached in Ocean Grove, New Jersey. Just
before I went to the pulpit I heard a repeated clicking noise.
I was told that the organist was pulling out the stops. It
made me wonder what God could do with me if I pulled out
all the stops!

Yes, we do live in a hopeless time. Praise God. Perhaps
now we can find our hope in him. Yes, the diminutive gods
are dead. Thank God! Long live the Lord!

CHAPTER 8

The Charismatic Motto: Let It Happen!

> "It is not for you to know times or seasons which the Father has fixed by his own authority. But you shall receive power when the Holy Spirit has come upon you."—Acts 1:7-8

My close friends tell me that they can always tell when I am insecure or uneasy. They tell me that I lower my voice in dramatic, ministerial intonation. The deeper and more ponderous I become the more they know that something is wrong and that I am depending more on talent than trust.

What about you? What is the telltale, undeniable sign for you that you've tightened up and are unsure? What do you do or say that makes it obvious to those around you that your sphincter muscle has tightened and you've taken over the management of the universe? Do you become loquacious or solemn and silent? Or do you become frenetic in overactivity, defensive in your attitudes? Do you lose sleep, overeat, or have to be in charge? What is it for you? We all have a way.

One thing we all share is a desire to control not only what's happening to us right now, but also what will happen in the future. Whether this is caused by an overly disciplined puberty, a fear of failing, or an overcompensation for being disorganized or disorderly, the result is the same. We march to the cadences of those demanding drill sergeants—planning, programming, and permanence. It's difficult to "hang loose," relax, and let life happen.

I have a friend from the Philippines who ends our visits with some words which are not only in a foreign language but also communicate a way of life foreign to most of us. I'm not sure it's any easier for the people in the Philippines even when it's said in their own tongue. He says, *"Bahala na!"* This means "leave it to God!" Great saying—but difficult to live. That does about as much for us as the clip jargon of "let go, let God!" All of our lives we have been taught to be responsible, to follow through, and to get things done. Control becomes a way of life. You and I are desperately afraid of things getting out of our determined direction, and we manipulatively move the people of our lives about on the checker board of our planned strategy so that we will never be checkmated by the unexpected.

I admire people like Charles Kettering who said, "I expect to spend the rest of my life in the future, so I want to be reasonably sure of what kind of future it's going to be. That's my reason for planning." I agree! There is no person who has more one-day, next-year, five-year, and ten-year plans than I have for both myself and my church. But the disturbing question is: When is our planning telling God what I want him to do and when is it catching his dream?

Do you share with me the difficulty in finding the intersection between trying and trusting, working and willing God's will, planning and praying? Frankly, I wish I knew what God was up to in his next move. I wish I could always outguess him in my evolving destiny. When is trusting the future to God irresponsibility and copping out of our human responsibility?

I hope you share in the comfort I now take in the fact that there were eleven men of remarkable historical stature who shared our problem. They could have been called the "Edgy Eleven." When we read the first half of the first chapter of Acts, we are rather embarrassed for them. Did they know what they were saying?

Catch the insecurity, the compulsivity, the desire to be sure of every detail of the future! "Lord, will you at this time restore the kingdom to Israel?" Was this an affirmation of confidence in Jesus, an expression of commitment to whatever he would do, a passing bit of chitchat before the ascension cloud arrived? No, it was a question of fear, a desperate fear, that things were getting out of their control and observable touch. They were nationalistic to the end. Would Jesus establish his earthly reign right now?

What a disturbingly dumb question! We want to run up Mount Olive and interrupt the disciples and say: No! Don't ask that now! What poor timing! With all you've been through with the Master, in the light of all he's done, in consideration of all the amazing surprises of his resurrection and appearances to you, in the context of all he's taught you about the kingdom, in view of his promise of the Holy Spirit, how can you worry about the future?

But then we pull back, for suddenly it dawns on us that if we had been there, we would have asked the same question. Then the realization deepens. We know so much more than those desperate disciples. We look at Olivet through the doors of the upper room at Pentecost and two thousand years of spectacular expansion of the mission of the kingdom. But we are still asking the same question about the affairs of our life. "Lord, what's next? What are you going to do? What will happen to us?"

You would think that instead of a question, the disciples would have given a shout of jubilant exultation. "Lord, thanks for all you have done for us: your call of inept people like us; your death for us and our sin; your resurrection and manifestation that nothing's too big for God; your appearances to us as a living Lord in those days since the resurrection; your wonderfully adequate dealing with our fears and doubts. Problems are possibilities now; we are ready for anything! The future is our trusted companion with you in charge!"

Not so! Instead an uneasy question exposing not only misunderstanding of Jesus' essential message about the kingdom of God, but also revealing ambivalence about the future. Too harsh? After all, think what those eleven had been through! Yes, but think of what they had been given!

According to Luke's account in the first verses of Acts, Jesus had "presented himself alive." The Greek means he actually lodged with them. And what did he talk about—the kingdom. We are sure that what he said was consistent with his persistent teaching: the kingdom of God is his rule and power within them, amongst them, and coming in society as they lived under his guidance and direction. He boldly told them that they would be baptized with the Holy Spirit. That's how he would come to them. He had dwelt with them; soon he would dwell in them. He would never be more present in power than when he was absent in body. That's the assurance of the ascension. He had to leave them to come again. That's how he deals with us. Whenever we have everything worked out, become secure in our relationship with him, get our ideas about him into tight compartments of religious observance, he leaves, but only to return in a dimension of power we never believed possible. He will never allow us to rest at any stage of growth. "It is best for you that I go away," he told the disciples. It has always been thus, so that we will trust him and not our plans for him in our future.

But the disciples could not perceive what he was trying to tell them. There was a grid, a lattice screen over their minds, interwoven with their expectation of a spectacular theocracy. Their hearing filter kept out anything but the hope of restoration of the past glory of Israel. Jesus wanted to shift the emphasis from the restoration of the past to the transformation of the present. All fear of the future should then have vanished. But it didn't.

In a way, I'm happy that the disciples reacted the way they did, for Jesus' answer to them is a three part prescription for our worry-weary, future-laden hearts. He tells us: (1) that's none of your business; (2) you will be given what you need; (3) to do what you must in each situation or circumstance.

The first part of Jesus' bold answer catches the decisive deliberateness of his response. "It's not for you to know the times or the seasons which the Father has fixed by his own authority." What he was saying was that it's not for us to know, since it's not our concern! Keep in mind that the subject is the kingdom. We are concerned only about God's rule in our hearts, our relationships, and our responsibilities. The kingdom is always quadralateral: in our inner being; with the people of our lives; in our material possessions; and with the world in which we live. Thus, it covers all dimensions of our existence in the present.

Now all questions about the future are set in bold relief: What's going to happen to me? How are things ever going to work out? What will happen in my family, my job, my society?

It's not for us to know! But what if we did know? Have you ever had inside, esoteric insight into something few others know? Often we respond, "I wish I would never have known!" The mercy of God is expressed in that he never overloads the circuits of today's concerns with knowledge of what will happen in the future.

But something else is hinted at in Jesus' answer. Our rigid, predestinarian forefathers would be disturbed by this, but I really believe that God is with us in a continuing creation. Why else should we pray? We are cocreators with him. The future is evolving. It is obscured by both the treacherous and good things people may do to affect our future and by what he can do with both the best and worst that happens to us.

This is what the psalmist described. "The Lord is my shepherd, I shall not want . . . he restores my soul . . . even though I walk through the valley of the shadow of death, thou art with me." What does this lead to for trusting the future? "Surely goodness and mercy shall follow me all the days of my life; and I shall dwell in the house of the Lord for ever." Our only task is to discover the Lord's guidance for goodness and mercy now. Our future in his house is his response and reward.

There is no question that we can affect our own future by careful planning and diligent preparation. We are all becoming what we envision; our goals determine what we achieve; our planning affects our progress. That's being responsible. But what about the unexpected that sometimes maximizes our dreams far beyond what we could ever have envisioned or the dreadful that dashes our hopes on the rocks of abhorred eventualities?

For example, if I would have known what God had in mind for me in the future I could not have taken the pressure of the amazing destiny he has provided. His interventions, the special gifts, the surprises in people and unexpected turn of events, the surge of strength and wisdom I never expected, were never planned by me. He has always exceeded my boldest expectations. How can I even thank him? But I have known, also, the uninvited guests of pain, loss, and disappointment. I cannot explain them.

Recently, I lost one of my best friends and fellow workers. Few people I have known were as effective with people as Jim Ferguson. He incarnated the affirmation and encouragement of the Lord. He was part of my dream for the future of my church. How can I rationalize the loss of a crucial teammate like Jim? He was strategic to my plan. I had hopes for him right up to his retirement and beyond, for as many years as he had strength to give his winsome, manly leadership. But because we are all human and physically mortal, does that mean that Jim and I should not have planned and dreamed right up to the end? The last time I saw him, his final remark was, "I can't wait to tell you of a new plan I have for a fresh phase of my work." That's life!

Yes, we must plan and scheme and dream and have visions right up to the end. But these expectations must never become our gods. The Lord will not reorder the universe around our organization flow chart or timetable. You see, there must be a balance; plan as if everything depended on us to catch and implement the Lord's plans; and then trust as if everything depended on him. Then when interruptions, changes, disappointments, or amazing unexpected delights come our way, we know that God has taken the best that we could plan and done the maximum to perpetuate his overall purpose for us.

But what about those tragedies and disappointments? They require a retrospective look. When we surrender them to him, he can use them for our growth and for his glory. The only difficulties which have ever damaged me are the ones I was determined to solve in my own strength. I have only two alternatives when calamity strikes: trust him and allow him to use it or hang on to it and allow it to destroy me. That's the decision of raw faith the disciples had to make when Jesus asked them, "Will you, too, go away?" My answer is Peter's: "Lord, to whom shall we go? You alone have the words of eternal life!" That frees us to ask: What's the best or worst that can happen to those for whom death is defeated, eternal life has begun, the indwelling Christ has been given, and the power of prayer has been unleashed. So why not make the future a friend?

Now I don't see that there is any way that that can possibly happen until we have the assurance that we will have adequate resources to meet whatever happens in the future. That's why the second aspect of Jesus' answer to the disciples is so liberating. "You shall receive power when the Holy Spirit comes upon you." He offers nothing less than the living presence of God himself. The disciples were to receive all the equipment for reality they needed. If we find the accounts of the miraculous events of the early church remarkable, it is because of the remedial power of the Holy Spirit, Christ in the present tense—the creating, sustaining Lord of all life. Our confidence is that we will never drift beyond God's care and he will never leave us unequipped to deal with the complexities that happen to and around us.

It is mysterious, wonderful, and yet beyond explanation. I know it to be true for me. Without the Holy Spirit, God's present power, I could not think clearly his thoughts after him nor have his insights into human need. I could not preach without the Holy Spirit. I have never convinced anyone to become a Christian. The Spirit does the work in the human mind and heart. He prepares people, gives the gift of faith, starts them on the new life, nourishes them to maturity. My task is to preach the Word viably, personally, relationally. I would not dare counsel anyone without the conviction that the Spirit is present. I am constantly driven to prayer about our future here as a church. That's why long periods of prayer and meditation have become more crucial than eating and sleeping. Without study, times of honest, corrective fellowship with trusted fellow adventurers and even deepening dependence, I could not go on!

This is where I have found the perfect blend between human potential and divine power, human planning and Spirit perception. With the Holy Spirit we can open the future to God and bring more of our direction within his general and specific guidance. We can leave the ouija board of wishful guessing behind and trust God to enable us to want what he wants for us.

But even then, events and circumstances will make us wonder if we missed his guidance. Sometimes we will have actually misjudged altogether. But even then, we are not beyond his power. Now his love comes in the shape of forgiveness and a new chance, a new beginning, and new growth. What a great God! Indeed, happy are the people whose God is the Lord!

The last aspect of Jesus' answer is the most healing. There is a final step in any learning, an ultimate interpretation of conceptual truth in experiential realization of the Spirit. Jesus said, "And you shall be my witnesses." Verbalization will mean comprehension. Sharing with others will bring solidification of the truth of what God is saying to us and doing with us in any situations. Wherever the disciples go—Jerusalem, Samaria, the uttermost parts of the earth—there is where they must witness, not just to the concepts of his acts and message, but also to what they were discovering of his presence and power in their personal lives. He begins at the center of the disciples' known world and reaches out to all creation. We shall be his witnesses and realize all that any event in the future has to teach us and has for us to communicate to others.

The witness of the early church was about the acts of the Holy Spirit in the circumstances of their life. It was their witness to what the Lord had done in their problems, pains, perturbations that won the world. When the future unfolded unexpected packages of success or victory, then witness was to Christ and the power of the Holy Spirit. When events turned against them, it was a new opportunity to share what God could do in difficulties.

Note also that the early Christians were always responding to unplanned developments of God's grace. It was only in retrospect that they theorized about what had happened. The Holy Spirit was not only within them, but also way out ahead, preparing the way. It was not a planned five-year strategy that they sent Barnabas and John to lay hands on the new Christians in Samaria. It was in response to the gift of God that they did the next appropriate thing. Peter did not have Cornelius as point four in his strategy. The gospel mission to the Gentile world was the furthest thing from his mind. In preparation God gave the vision, the power, and then the unbelievable expansion into the Gentile world.

Paul wanted to go to Rome. He planned ahead. But he had no idea of what God had in mind for that long eventful journey. It takes six chapters of Acts to record all the serendipities! Planning and trust equalized God's interventions and unexpected blessings. Christianity is more than a point of arrival; it's a present point of departure. Being in Christ is more than a secure harbor. A harbor does more than dock ships safely away from the open sea. It is also a place from which ships sail out into the restless sea that has the unbelievable red sunsets of peace, but also the storms of tumult.

What is true for us as individuals is true for the church. We are not a funeral parlor to embalm the past; we are a fellowship of Copernican thinkers and dreamers who realize that the best days are ahead. Our task is no less exciting than that of Copernicus, who said and proved the world revolved around the sun. The challenge to us is to witness to the fact that the future orbits around the Son of God, not around our little world of calculated determination.

We feel like Edmund Wilson in his impression of Mitchelet's *History of France:*

> There is no book which makes us feel when we have finished it that we have lived through and known with such intimacy so many generations of men. And it makes us feel something more: that we ourselves are the last chapter of the story, and that the last chapter is for us to create.

One correction: the next chapter is for God to write. All he needs is you and me to be open pages to write upon. The other day I discovered some amazing little books at a book binder. They were beautifully bound in leather and looked like carefully bound volumes of wisdom. Everything on the outside gave them the appearance of scholarly volumes, which would enhance the shelves of any well read person's library. But inside, all the pages were blank! I bought one and have used it to record what God is teaching me each day and what he reveals of his plan for the future of my life. The future is still to be written, and I am expectantly ready!

Now I can say *"Bahala na!"* with new vigor and viability. Leave it to God. But what shall we leave to him? Irresponsible, negligent refusal to dream with the future as a friend? No! What we leave with him are the plans he has drafted and imparted. However he wants to amend them or revise them as we move into the future is up to him.

That's not a bad offer. He created the universe, made the wonder of you and me, stooped to the cross and rose to the resurrection, and filled the emptiness in our hearts. Not a bad track record! So why not let it happen?

CHAPTER 9

Power to You!

"Did you receive the Holy Spirit when you believed?"—Acts 19:2

It had been a good lunch and a fine time for catching up. Amazingly enough, I had had no agenda. There was no job I wanted the man to take, no money I wanted to raise, no cause I wanted him to support. We had been friends for years, and it was good to be together with no other purpose than to enjoy our friendship. Yet, as the conversation flowed, I felt a subtle depression in my friend, a business-as-usual attitude, a "ho-humness" about his deepest relationships. There were no profound problems, no crushing crises to be dealt with, just a pervading blandness. We recalled together the time when he had begun the Christian life when life was not so placid for him. Now I felt him avoiding any deep conversation. We ended the lunch with pleasantries, and my friend walked me to the parking lot. I must confess that I did not give a lot of thought to my parting words. But what I said was more than a simplistic shibboleth to him. "Power to you," I said and reached for my car door. That seemed to be the opening he had been waiting for. "That's just what I need!" he said intently, "power is the one thing I lack." He then went on to tell me that he had lost the joy and peace he had felt when he first became a Christian, years before.

Then he began to talk about the things I felt he had wanted to talk about all through the luncheon. What he said was a remarkable description of lots of us. "I believe in God and attend church fairly regularly, but something's missing. I can remember how good I felt when I turned my problems over to God years ago. But very little has happened since. I just don't seem to feel God's power the way others do. I try to do what's right, try to be a good husband and father, work hard at my job, but it's not any fun. When you said 'power to you' I felt a lightning bolt inside me. I guess that's what I need—power!"

In this man I felt and heard the plight of so many church people. He believed in God, but he was not personal, and therefore his life was powerless.

The other day, I spent a relaxed time with a group of clergy in another city. They were a discouraged, depleted lot. Their dreams for their churches had diminished into drab routine. They had preached, organized, scheduled, challenged, and saw little evidence of vigor and vitality in their people. Some suggested that it was the beginning of summer and people were tired of organized efforts and wanted a vacation from churchmanship. Others picked up the dreary note, hoping that a summer of rest would bring new life. Others were not sure that they wanted to try to infuse new life with another year of planned programs, slick brochures to get people to do what should come naturally, and stirring messages which stirred no one. The thing I sensed in these men was the same thing I noted in my old friend. The bland religious life we live is not consistent with, but a contradiction to the amazing life Jesus revealed and offers to us.

Now, the remarkable thing about these two incidents in the span of two weeks is that my luncheon friend is a member of one of those pastors' congregations. As I flew home, I reflected on the coincidence. Who was to blame? The church member said he wasn't getting much out of his church. The pastor said he couldn't seem to infuse life in the spiritually satisfied and unadventuresome congregation. Both to blame? Yes, but more importantly both needed the same thing—power.

All of us are alike: we are adrift without the Holy Spirit—the only undepletable store of power to live the Christian life, the only reservoir of spiritual energy, the only source of personal contact with God, the only continuing renewal of joy and excitement about and for daily living.

Paul's question to a band of followers of John the Baptist on the road to Ephesus is the central question for us and the church as a whole. These men had been baptized into a religion of repentance and renunciation. They had not heard of the good news of the gospel and were bound in their own religious efforts to please God. They belonged to a memorial society for a dead leader. Their religion gave them neither might nor strength. They had a heritage without hope, a loyalty without liberation, a purpose without a presence, a vision without a victory. Paul's bold, incisive question was: Did you receive the Holy Spirit when you believed? Their answer was, like many of us would have to reply, "No, we have never heard that there is a Holy Spirit." The main difference with us is that we probably have heard the words "Holy Spirit" so often that we no longer hear. The startling fact of contemporary Christianity is that so few Christians, fine church people, have gone no further in discovering the amazing resources of God than those dutiful disciples of John who were bound up in the ineffective compulsivity of religious zeal, a life built around renunciation without an inner reformation.

I can imagine the paces Paul put them through. He told them of God's love and forgiveness in Christ and the Cross, the victory of the resurrection, but then, and never to be omitted, the present power of the Holy Spirit. Because he was not hampered by the rigid tri-theism which Christian history has clamped on our minds through theological formulations of the Trinity, he began where they were in their commitment to the righteousness and judgment of God taught by John. He then told them about what God did to make man right with himself through Christ the Immanuel, God with us. Can't you feel the rigor of his impelling words of explanation and witness of what Christ meant? Then he took them to the foot of the Cross and imparted to them the power of the blood of Christ for forgiveness and new life. Then we sense the quickening of his pace when he told about the open tomb and the resurrected Lord. He led them to the upper room and Pentecost and introduced them to the living Lord. Then his message must have been sealed with the wondrous invitation for them to receive the Holy Spirit. His message had proclaimed the three ways God has of being God: (1) creator, judge, and Lord of all; (2) incarnate Savior and redeemer of all; (3) indwelling presence and enabler of all. The disciples of John had only the first and, like many of us, needed to accept what God had done for them as Christ and Savior and would do in them as the Holy Spirit.

The result of that encounter was profound. They came to know the Holy Spirit as the life of God in their own souls. Vitality, excitement, contagion, charisma resulted. The experience of God's grace in Christ opened them to be the transmitters of that grace through the Holy Spirit. In Ephesus they shared what they had found and spread the liberating experience. They had moved from religion to life!

This account describes our condition, gives us the answer to our basic problems, and shows us what can happen to us. It gives us one essential truth about God and three undeniable insights about us: We learn what God is like and discover where we are, what we need, and what results we can expect.

The truth about God that we need to discover again is that the Holy Spirit was not an afterthought. The names of God all grow from a common root of man's experience. Creator, Judge, Redeemer, Father are all titles which describe aspects of the nature of God which people came to know in their experience of him. Jesus taught us that "God is a Spirit, that those who worship him must worship in Spirit and in truth. For such the Father seeks to worship him." He also taught that God is one. Each of the names of God do not represent a separate deity but aspects of one substance. It is the Holy Spirit who created the world, guided his people in knowing his nature, dwelt in Jesus Christ as Savior, raised him from the dead, and returned in present power. That's why we need to know the Holy Spirit!

First of all he is the presence of God—God in his approach to man. He came to us, in search of us, through the Holy Spirit. He knows us, loves us, and realizes our need for him. He will not let us go! There is no place we can hide from him, no condition into which we can fall that is too bad for him, and no defenses which are too strong for him. The first step of initiative love is always his. We are recipients of Joel's promise: "And in the last days it shall be, God declares, that I will pour out my Spirit upon all flesh." The only response we can make to that are the words of the psalmist, "Whither shall I go from thy Spirit?" And the plea, "Take not thy Holy Spirit from me." We scan the Scriptures, and the truth is plain: the Spirit is poured out, men are filled by the Spirit, and the Spirit abides with men.

Secondly, the Holy Spirit is the preparer—God in his internal access to us. Only the Holy Spirit can reach into the interior recesses of human personality, which are not open to us in our normal relationships with one another. He stimulates our desire to know him, awakens our conscience, reminds us of what he has done for us in Jesus Christ. Our Lord's promise is clear in this perspective: "He shall bring to your remembrance all that I have done for you." Because the Spirit is pure unmotivated love, he can move into the deepest areas of our hidden hearts. There he prepares us with a sense of our need, a realization of our impotence, a feeling of our futility, and a vision of our destiny. He prepares a way for the gospel, mediates the power of the gospel, gives the gift of faith to respond to the gospel, and provides the power to live the gospel.

Paul discerned the ministry of the Holy Spirit as preparer. In Romans 8:26-27 he says, "Likewise the Spirit helps us in our weakness; for we do not know how to pray as we ought, but the Spirit himself intercedes . . . for the saints according to the will of God." Our search for God is because he has been in search of us; our desire to know him is because he knows us already; our intellectual quest is because he has us in mind; our longing to know his will is because he has gone before us to prepare the very things he prompts us to ask.

That leads us to the third aspect of the Holy Spirit. He is propitiator—God in his redeeming activity in us. Our greatest problem is what to do with what we are and have done. Sin is separation, independence, and negativism. The most difficult thing for us to realize is the forgiveness and acceptance of God. Our self-justifying nature impells us to find some way of atoning for ourselves or making ourselves right. But no amount of hiding, covering, deceptive activity can heal the wound. We all feel it; we all suffer from the results of our rebellion. It is no easy task to get through to us. We can talk about grace, sing about it in our hymns, hear it preached endlessly, but to experience it and realize it is an impossible task for us. Unmerited love, a love we have done nothing to deserve or earn, cannot be realized by us either intellectually or emotionally. What is impossible for us is the propitiatory ministry of the Holy Spirit. He breaks us open with the love of the Cross and reorders the tissues of our brains to be able to conceive and then to grasp the alarming truth of amazing grace.

This explains why so many of us believe in Christ and yet live lives of guilt and frustration. Or what is equally wrong is that we may live lives of pious, self-generated, justification-through-activity human goodness, and highly polished personalities. Have you ever wondered why we could hear about a love that cannot be earned and then spend our lives trying to earn it? That's exactly why we need the Holy Spirit. He alone can tenderly force us to see ourselves as we are and then mediate the transforming power of the forgiving love of God. It is through the testimony of the Spirit as an inward experience of the soul that I realize that I am a child of God, that what Christ did was for me, that I am forgiven, and that I am reconciled forever.

We are now ready to see the ministry of the Holy Spirit as proprietor—God in his sanctifying authority over our lives. The Holy Spirit reorders our minds around the mind which was in Christ Jesus.

When I was a pastor in Winnetka, Illinois, I was given the use of a large mansion for study while the family was away. In response I was to be proprietor for the family in its absence. But, to my surprise, I was given a key to only the front door and the library. I had to be responsible for rooms which were locked to me! It was only after a few years, when the trust level had grown that I was given the keys to every room in the house. That's how we relate to the Holy Spirit. He is proprietor, but most of the rooms of our experience are closed to him. But we have the freedom to unlock all the rooms and let him live in us. He is God in residence. Paul said, "But it is God who establishes us . . . he has put his seal upon us and given us his Spirit in our hearts as a guarantee" (II Cor. 1:21-22).

What does he do if we give him all the keys? He heals the memories of the past. He is Lord of the subconscious. In the presence of his love, we can relive the harbored hurts. He takes the sting out of the wound. Then he exposes our values and priorities of the present. To have the mind of Christ through his Spirit is to be able to think his thoughts with discernment and insight. He shows us his goals for us and gives us his agenda and timing. We are changed into Christ-likeness from one degree of glory into another. He makes us like Jesus, in attitude, love, and graciousness.

How should we respond to this proprietory ministry of the Holy Spirit? If he knows us as we are, and we can hide nothing from him, then the only response we can give is moment by moment, day by day relinquishment. Paul knew what this meant. "If the Spirit of him who raised Jesus from the dead dwells in you, he who raised Jesus from the dead will give life to your mortal bodies also through his Spirit which dwells in you" (Romans 8:11).

The fourth aspect of the ministry of the Holy Spirit is personality—God in his assimilation of himself in man. The fruit of the Holy Spirit delineated by Paul in Galatians 5 is the description of the person of Jesus and the personality of the indwelt believer. Love, joy, peace, patience, kindness, goodness, faithfulness, gentleness, and self-control describe what our personalities are to be when inwardly motivated by the Spirit. That thought is a slippery rock for

most of us. We have been conditioned and patterned to
think that the true qualities of Christian personality are to
be developed by us to please God. Many of us were taught
that if you want to have God love you, you ought to be more
loving or patient or kind. We have missed the plain truth
that no one can have any of these qualities apart from the
Holy Spirit. We can simulate them for a time, but soon we
end up in pretending or frustration. The fruit of the Spirit,
the Christian personality, is always inadvertent. When you
focus on them they diminish; when you focus on Christ
through the gift of the Spirit, the result is that they grow in
us naturally. We can stop trying to be Christians and start
living the transferred life—life by the Holy Spirit. The result
will be authentic Christian personality.

The last dimension of the ministry of the Holy Spirit is
power—God in his appropriation of himself in us. The
power of God is an illusive thing we talk about a lot. I find it
helpful to consider the gifts of the Holy Spirit as the power
tools of God for our ministry. This power is for the extension
of the ministry of Christ through us. The needs in people
and our society bring forth the particular gift that is needed
to communicate Christ, do his will, and live obediently as
agents of change in society. The gifts are not for our
pleasure but for his purposes. Power is not a matter of
self-generation but of appropriation. It is not strenuous
activity but open hospitality to the Spirit's work in and
through us. Receptivity is the secret to divine energy.

These are three kinds of power needed by most of us in
our ministry. Intellectual power is given in the gifts of
wisdom and knowledge. God opens himself to us through
the Holy Spirit. He invades the thought pattern of our
minds and plants insight into his nature, plan, and purpose.
We can see things from his point of view. That's wisdom.
Knowledge is that wisdom in practical application to life.

The Holy Spirit is the Spirit of truth. He helps us see things as they are. His truth exposes the false and partial. We can understand. Intellectual capacity is multiplied and heightened. The brilliance of the Christian is a gift.

Spiritual power is rooted in the gift of faith. That same gift which enabled us to respond to God's love in Christ now empowers us to trust him in the needs and difficulties of life. All things are possible now because of the limitless resources of the Holy Spirit. Not all things are expeditious for his plans or timing, but they are all possible. That's why we must keep open to his guidance to know how to pray. He is the source of all healing; thus the person in whom he dwells has gifts for the healing of people's ills. We are given power to pray for the sick bodies, minds, emotions, relationships, and problems of people. Our healing services have given us undeniable evidence that the Holy Spirit is the healer. At the conclusion of the services the elders line up across the front of the chancel in the sanctuary, and people come forward for the laying on of hands. We have seen the Spirit of the impossible at work. The greatest result has been in the elders themselves who have felt the Holy Spirit surge through them for the healing of persons.

But the gift of healing must be coupled with the gift of miracles. This gift gives boldness and courage to trust God for his intervention. A miracle is not a denial of the laws of nature, but an affirmation of a higher law which supersedes natural limitations. Miracles are not limited to the spectacular realm of nature. We believe that the new life is the greatest miracle. A person under the control of the Holy Spirit is miraculous. In a world that is tightly bound in the limitations of human resources and capacities, we desperately need people who dare to believe that God is able. The gift of working miracles enables a person to say, "What does God want? Let's dare to pray for that!"

That's where the gift of working miracles and the gift of prophecy overlap. Let me stress that the "thus saith the Lord" quality of the prophetic Christian gives him the power to see what God is doing and desiring in a situation and be unreserved in obedience to that. This gift is desperately needed in the contemporary church. We need people who have taken time to discover the strategy of God revealed in the Scriptures and order our priorities around that. The gift of prophetic power is to communicate to others what the Holy Spirit has revealed as truth. I thank God for some of my friends who have this gift. They can see into the depths of problems and opportunities and sense what God is saying. They then can speak the truth they see with guileless sensitivity. That gift is available to all of us. Think of the goofs and mistakes, the wrong directions and the misfired shots which could be avoided if we were open to and dependent on this gift!

But here is also emotional power in the Holy Spirit. The emotions are channels through which the Holy Spirit moves through us to others. However, many of us are blocked and retarded emotionally. The psychological blows of life have made us cautious. Some have not been loved in a healthy, liberating way. To be able to give and receive emotional love is a great blessing. The gift of tongues is for emotional release. Since tongues are given primarily as a new language to praise God, we get an insight into the nature of this gift. Praise unlocks the emotions. It frees us up to recognize the wonders of God but also unbinds us to anticipate what God can do. When we praise in problems, we are open to receive God's strength as well as his answer. But sometimes our own language is inadequate, and we are overcome with a realization of the majesty and might of the love of God. It is at that point we are free to receive the Holy Spirit's praise to God through us. That's difficult for some of us intellectuals, but that's the point at which our arrogance is broken. The gift of tongues breaks out of our inner self, and we praise God in words beyond our own. The result is new emotional freedom to love with warmth and tenderness. That for me is the authentic test of tongues: that the gift results in evident new love for people and costly caring for their needs.

The power of the Holy Spirit is available to you and me now. Why do we insist on self-effort which like quicksand, the harder we struggle the more deeply we are mired in defeat. Paul gives two warnings: "Do not grieve the Holy Spirit" (Ephesians 4:30); "Do not quench the Spirit" (I Thessalonians 5:19). And then he gives an admonition: "Be filled with the Spirit" (Ephesians 5:18). That means more receptivity than activity; more hospitality than aggressiveness. But we can say no to the Holy Spirit so long that it's difficult to say yes. D. L. Moody was asked, "Who is the man who has caused you more problems than any other man you have met?" He answered, "D. L. Moody!" We are often our own worst enemies when it comes to receiving the Holy Spirit. We resist what we need the most.

The real reason may be that we don't need the Holy Spirit! Perhaps we have hammered down life's possibilities so cautiously that we don't need his power. That leads to a question. What are you attempting that could not be done without the gifts of the Holy Spirit? What adventuresome risks have you taken that are utterly impossible without his power? Where are you out in the deeps over your head where only he could sustain and save?

There's the key! The reason we know so little of the Holy Spirit is that we have attempted so little of the exciting promises of Jesus.

We have come full circle back to my luncheon friend. His bland, uncourageous brand of cautious Christianity had blocked out the need for the Holy Spirit's power. But he was not satisfied! Praise God for that. The Holy Spirit would not leave him alone. Nor will he leave us comfortable and complacent. Don't you sense a feeling of emptiness, inadequacy and insufficiency sweeping over you? That's his gift so he can give you his power.

If you believed that all power would be given you this next week, what would you attempt? What reconciliations would you try? What restitution would you perform? What bold move of courage would you dare? What exciting adventure for God would you contemplate?

Do you feel the reservation cap flip off, the flood gates open, the reservoir filling up?

Did you receive the Holy Spirit when you believed that with God all things were possible? Power to you!

CHAPTER 10

The Great Holdout

Not long ago there was a meeting of Satan and his lieutenants to devise a plan on how to undermine the dynamic ministry and mission of my church. Satan gathered all his best demonic emissaries for a briefing session to develop a strategy. As all the cunning characters huddled closely to the throne of disgrace in the kingdom of darkness, Satan outlined the agenda with a pervasive inclusiveness that gave all of them the sense that they were going to be a part of the planning of the scheme he already had in mind.

Listen closely as he states the problem. "The church has been the bane of our efforts to destroy the kingdom of the enemy for seventy years now. Their missionaries get in our way all over the world, the theological students that have come out of their congregations are now pastoring some of the strongest churches in America; the thousands of people who have become Christians have defeated us on too many fronts; they have preached Christ with so much power that it has been a model; and the movements that have been started there cripple us all over the world! Look at what we have allowed to happen! The church must be stopped. I think now is our chance! Now is the time to divide and conquer. How do you think we can do it?"

Immediately the demons jump up raising their hands for Satan's attention, shouting, "We know, we know!"

The patron demon of destruction is recognized first.

"I've got it! Send another earthquake!"

Satan shakes his head. "That won't do, Destruction! What I know of those people, they will find some other place to meet that's even bigger, and the adversity will swell their crowds!"

The demon on intransigence speaks next. "Listen to me. I have the infallible plan. If you all will help me we can accomplish it. I will try to get into Ogilvie's mind and make him move too fast. We'll block out the Holy Spirit's gift of timing and discernment and get him to change everything. Then we can get a slogan going among the people. How about this: 'We never did it that way before!'"

Again Satan shakes his head. "Sorry, that may work in some churches, but it won't work here. They've been known for innovation and new ventures. That's always been our problem with them. They are far too flexible an enemy for that. No, those people are too wise not to believe that customs and heritage are worthy of trust. That won't do either."

The demon of denominational criticism speaks next. "I know; we can remind the people of all the things the denomination does that they don't like. We can build up their cultural and political loyalties against the enemy and have them pull out because they don't like what the General Assembly does. Keep reminding them of political pronouncements, student riots, and all that!"

Satan seems exasperated at the lack of creativity. "Demon of Denominational Criticism, won't you ever learn that that has worked on hundreds of churches, but it won't

do for that church. You forget that they see themselves as a
leader in that denomination. They speak out when they
disagree and are trying to shape its future. They bought into
the enemy's strategy of change from within rather than
criticism from without.

The demon of discouragement has been quiet. His dark,
gloomy face has been deep in pensive thought. He speaks
deliberately as if he has a devilish, dastardly idea.

"Let's take the despair of the times and infuse it into the
church. America is in a terrible state. All of the institutions
are crumbling under our pressure. Let's make them think
that whatever they do, it won't make any difference."

Satan shows some enthusiasm about this. "Now you're
getting close. But you're not on yet. I can't understand why
you have missed the obvious. The only way we can destroy
that church is to beat them at their own game. We must
overemphasize a good and destroy the best. Let's take one
of the greatest strengths of that church and use it to sap its
strength. What's the one thing that church has always
stood for—Individual salvation and sanctification. That's
why they've grown; they told people that they could know
the enemy personally, and that he would give them power
for their lives. They even believe that their eternal life
begins now and lasts forever. We've got to stop that!"

"Here's the way. Let's convince them that being with the
enemy has nothing to do with their relationship with their
fellow church members. Get them to believe that caring
about each other and their church is an unnecessary
addendum to their faith. If we can make them think that
the church is for what they get out of it, we will have
softened them up for the kill. The more we can emphasize
their own piety and get them to be uninvolved and
uncommitted to the other parts of the enemy's message
about the church as his body, we will have them. Then,

don't you see, the kind of dynamic church which introduced them to the faith will be weakened. Get them to stop·
being concerned about study and fellowship. Encourage
them to be happy in the enemy and cut down their giving.
Then we can get some of those outreach programs cut out,
bring some of those missionaries back home where they
belong and stop that church in its tracks! Remember, make
separative individualism a god, deify personal salvation, and
block out loyalty to the church. Keep them away from the
passage of the enemy's message about his church at all
costs! Ridicule Paul's idea of all parts of the body fitting
together with an irreplaceable function. Debunk all that
stuff about rejoicing and caring together and carrying each
other's burdens. If you can, and this will be difficult, make a
new order—call it the H.O.P.—Holy Order of Parapathetics. Plant the idea that there may be another church
where they can hear the gospel and satisfy their own
needs without getting involved. Then, demons, we'll have·
them! Our onslaught will be called 'operation holdout.'
You are now members of the mafia of equivocation. Your
motto is 'Prestige and privilege without price.' What we
almost accomplished with Ananias and Sapphira we can
do here."

That apocryphal story may seem like a figment of my
overactive imagination, but I wonder. The more I study our
text for today describing the great holdout of Ananias and
Sapphira, the more convinced I am that it expresses, not
only the greatest threat which has existed for the church
through the ages, but also the most subtle and serious
strategy of equivocation which confronts us today. Satan's
attention is drawn only to powerful churches which preach
Christ and relate to people in a liberating experience of
being part of the people of God. Since his lust is for
anonymity, I believe he should be exposed, and we should

see how we can become part of his strategy without
knowing it.

Some expositional background is helpful. The early
church was distinguished for the quality of commitment of
its members, not only to Christ but also to each other. They
shared what they had with each other out of love for Christ.
Peter's word to the lame beggar outside the Beautiful Gate
in Jerusalem marks this quality. The man asked for help;
Peter's response was "What I have I give you." The early
Christians believed that what they possessed was not theirs
but Christ's and, therefore, should be shared unreservedly
with the church.

Barnabas became famous in the fellowship because he
sold his lands and possessions and laid the proceeds before
the apostles for use among his fellow believers. That's when
Ananias and Sapphira became instruments of division and
disunity. They wanted the same adoration and acclaim
Barnabas received but at a bargain price. They conceived a
plan to sell a piece of property and create the impression
that they would give the whole proceeds to the church.
With carefully honed hypocrisy they folded up a portion of
the money in a napkin, and with dramatic self-glorifying,
attention-arresting flourish, Ananias entered the upper
room where the church gathered and placed it at Peter's
feet.

The battle between Satan and the Holy Spirit for the life
of the church was on! But Peter's gift of discernment
outdistanced Ananias' equivocation. He could tell that
Ananias' overacting, his egregious language, and his
sticky spirituality betrayed a great hoax. With cutting
clarity he sliced to the very heart of the deceit.

"Ananias, why has Satan filled your heart to lie to the Holy Spirit
and keep back part of the proceeds of the land? While it
remained unsold, did it not remain your own? And, after it was

sold, was it not at your disposal? How is it you have contrived this deed in your heart? You have not lied to men but to God" (Acts 5:3-4).

The point was this: selling what people had and giving it to the church was not a qualification of membership. Giving was to be motivated by love for the Master and his people. Ananias's sin was that he wanted to pretend a quality of life to get recognition, prestige, and popularity. Peter knew that if that type of equivocation became the model of the church's life, the demise of the church's glory and power would not be far off. The growth of that kind of hypocrisy had to be cut at the root. Pretension, posturing, and play-acting would pollute the whole fellowship.

The exposure was more than Ananias could take. He was seized by an excruciating guilt trauma which his heart would not tolerate. The church knew him for what he was: a liar and a cheat, a hypocrite who had held out on God and his people. This produced such a convulsion within him that he swayed and then fell dead at the apostles' feet, his gasping breath sounding the death rattle and his lifeless eyes gazingly fixed on the napkin filled with his Judas offering at the Apostle Peter's feet. He was carried off and buried.

Sapphira's fate was not any better. Three hours later she came into the room. Peter gave her every opportunity to honestly and openly admit what she had encouraged her husband to do. Again the same pretense and fictitious faithfulness, and once again Peter's decisive exposure. Then came the knowledge of Ananias's fate, and her own guilt seizure caused her own death. She too was carried away and buried. And fear came upon the whole church. Nothing could have dramatized the mutual responsibility of Christians to one another more than what had happened.

Our reflection on this event may cause us to wonder why

this story needed to be told by Luke in his account of the birth and growth of the church in Acts. We wonder if the punishment fits the crime. By our standards, Ananias's giving practices were very admirable. We'd like more people who would sell their property and give the church a handsome portion. But I believe the story stands as a vivid account of the church's first confrontation with the attack of Satan upon the vitals of its existence. He could not destroy the church from without through the persecution or criticism of the Jewish leaders or the Roman powers. His only chance was to destroy from within. If he could multiply the hypocrisy of Ananias in the membership of the church, the virulent poison of spiritual dishonesty would flow in the blood stream of the body of Christ, the church.

But what does a story like that have to say to us? Just this: we all can be instruments of Satan in pretending to a piety which is not real and viable. We can try to have a private relationship with Christ which is not accountable to the fellowship. We can withhold our affirmation and enthusiasm until the church is what we think it should be. We can resist movement and growth in ministry and mission by withholding our support and involvement while at the same time pretending enthusiasm and appreciation.

The great holdout is based on several fallacious assumptions and has several frightening implications. As biblical Christians we cannot tear this portion of Acts out of our Bibles. We must stand under its judgment and be instructed by its message. When we try to get hold of the meaning of this passage, suddenly we realize that it has gotten hold of us.

First the great holdout was based on the desire to have prestige and privilege without a price. Ananias and Sapphira wanted recognition without responsibility. Essentially we are infected with the same problem. When we reflect thoughtfully on all we have been given, we are amazed. We have been loved, accepted, and forgiven. Our Lord has called us to be his people. Individually he has given us the gift of faith to respond to the gospel. In Christ we are the recipients of grace for an abundant life now and with the assurance of eternal life forever. His intervening providence protects and provides. The serendipities of his love fill our difficulties with hope and new beginnings. He will not let us go! Our church is the source of our birth, growth, and nurture in a truly exciting life.

But not without a price! Unreservedness, abandoned wholeheartedness, complete commitment is the price of privilege. The great holdout develops when we want all that Christ has to give without surrender to his guidance and direction for our response. We try to manipulate him when we hold back our energies, our love, our possessions, and our giving while maintaining the impression that we belong to him.

The price of privilege in Christ is always spelled out relationally. It's true in marriage, the family, and among our friends. We enjoy the resources of love and comfort from the people our Lord has entrusted to us. We are part of the great holdout when we deny these people around us the warmth of love, the stimulation of encouragement, and the dynamic of affirmation they need. We become like the Vermont farmer who said to his wife, "Sara, you mean so much to me that sometimes it is more than I can stand not to tell you." Love-starved people are all around us. We thoughtlessly assume the benefits they provide us without the costly caring required. We are proud of the image-building influence a spouse, a child, or a friend can afford us, but hold back the one gift we have to give: ourselves.

The same is true of the church. Many of us are proud of the heritage of our churches. We are honored to be a part of its membership and leadership. It is here that many of us have been introduced to the joy and power of Christ. Our spiritual gamesmanship develops when we withhold ourselves and our involvement. We can try to maintain an outward piety of a previously discovered power when inwardly we are measuring out as little as we can to keep up the image. It has been said that the basic difference between a politician and a statesman is that the former uses public office for personal advantage while the latter treats his office as a trusteeship for the public good. The same is true of church members. Some use membership for what they can get out of it, while others use it for making available to others what they have experienced.

This is based on the second distorted assumption of the great holdout. Ananias and Sapphira believed they could have Christ without the church. They thought that their faith was a separatistic, individualistic vertical affair. Their privatism led to spiritual sickness. They believed they could compromise with Christ because they did not have to be accountable to the church. They were the benefactors of a whole breed of contemporary Christians who have only one third of the gospel.

Jesus Christ lived, died, and was raised for our individual salvation, our incorporation into his body, the church, and in ministry. We cannot have one without the other. The word ecclesia, church, means to be called out, called together, and called into mission. Jesus died, not only for our personal redemption, but also to create a people, the new Israel, solidified by the new convenant in his blood. Our problem today is that we want Christ without commitment to his church and involvement in his mission in the world. I find no such dichotomy in the Scriptures. Jesus was profoundly concerned about his disciples' relationship with one another and the birth of his church as the provisional demonstration of his eternal intention for all creation. He is concerned about what we are as a church as he is about our individual relationship with him.

The alarming problem is that many of us want to be inspired and uplifted for our private walk with Jesus without responsibility for the church, which exists to communicate that power. It's like going to a concert. We enjoy the conductor and his interpretation of the music but have little or no concern about the people seated around us. We come to get what we want and leave as soon as we can.

Satan's legion of parapathetics are swelled in number by people who want to be where there is great music and preaching to be enjoyed. We wander from church to church looking for where the action is. We are spellbound by one preacher after another but become strangely cool and critical whenever the involvement crunch comes. When attendance demands putting our lives on the line to faithfully sort out what it means to be an obedient disciple in the other two-thirds of the gospel, it's amazing how negative we can become as we strike our tents in search of the next thrilling episode in personal piety.

Now we all know too much about dead and dying churches in America where churchianity has been more important than Christianity, where people are more loyal to a church and its customs than to Christ. That's not what I am talking about. My concern is for the church that proclaims the wonders of personal life in Christ and neglects the Master's message about the awesome responsibility to be a giving, daring part of an innovating, experimental, evolving, emerging church of the New Testament. The church must always be both: a place where individuals meet the Beloved and pay the price of being the beloved community.

The problem with Ananias and Sapphira was that they

did not think through what would happen to the church if everyone enjoyed the same holdout. Luke would have had very little more to write about the expansion of Christianity if their dishonesty of duality pervaded the church. That's why Peter was so deliberately decisive.

But you and I must ask the same question. To what extent is my attitude and responsibility in the church an expression of the infection of Satan or the inspiration of the Holy Spirit? And if my own feelings and commitment were multiplied in all members, what kind of church would we have? To what extent have I been to my brothers and sisters in Christ in the church what Christ has been to me? Remember Jesus' acid test: "By this shall men know that you are my disciples, that you have love for one another." The kingdom he proclaimed was to be within, in the midst, and to be spread in the world.

Our holdout is often calculated by our judgments. We are all strong people who want things in keeping with our prejudices and preconceptions. Our evading excuses often come when our wills are thwarted. We withhold our enthusiasm until we hear our tune played to our tempo on our instrument. We forget what an orchestra might sound like with only one kind of instrument. The genius of the church is the unity of diversity which comes when we pray for Christ's direction together.

The vision which our Lord has given us is to provide a church which is inclusive by its variety. We want a feast of love which is like a smörgasbord. We are all hungry, but we may not all want the same dishes. If everyone is forced to eat all the same food, we will lose the delightful freedom Christ wants for all of us. But that we feast together enjoying our host and each other is the undeniable challenge to all of us.

We must never confuse creative dissent with the great

holdout. A truly great church must always be open to correction by its own members. That's how we grow. It's by the blending of our uniqueness and particular convictions that we are honed into the sharpness for Christ needed in the church today. But involvement and support, coupled with true unbreakable loyalty to each other in Christ is the price of admission to critical insight. The holdout comes when we withhold these until things are the way we want them. That's a luxury no member can afford!

Thirdly, the great holdout is based on an underestimation of the power of Satan. Peter asked Ananias, "Why has Satan put it into your heart to lie to the Holy Spirit?" I am sure that Ananias did not think that Satan had prompted his scheme. A clever business deal to have the best of both worlds of recognition and financial security, yes—but not the ploy of Satan.

The other day I talked with a famous general who was distinguished in the Pacific during World War II. I asked him the secret of his success. His answer came quickly: "I never underestimated the enemy and always kept my supply routes open."

He was like Peter! Peter had had his own scrapes with Satan. He had been told that he was on Satan's side when he tried to dissuade Jesus from his mission, he had denied his Lord when Satan had tried to sift him like wheat, he had battled with Satan against Christ's control of his life. That's the reason he could discern what was happening to poor Ananias. He knew that his soul was the battleground for Satan and the Holy Spirit. He also realized that the church was the focus of satanic attack. He gave no gentle permissive scolding. Instead he confronted Satan and threw the lie in his face.

It's true for us also. Behind the pride of selfishness of our great holdout is the power of evil. There are times that

Christ must say of all of us what he said to Peter, "Get thee behind me Satan!" Often our attitudes and manipulations are the direct result of underestimating Satan's power to destroy us and undercut the church. He is not concerned with drab, dull churches. His attack is always on the members of powerful churches that are changing people and society.

That leaves us with a disturbing question. Is there any holdout in me? Could it be that I am a part of Satan's mafia of equivocation in any way?

The last thing I want to say is that the great holdout is the cause of spiritual death. Ananias and Sapphira died of guilt seizure. But there could have been a creative moment of healing. It was because they could not bear exposure that they died. All they would have needed to do was to admit their failure and the healing stream of Christ's mercy would have flowed forth from the Apostles and their fellow church members. Honesty is the antidote to hypocrisy. But Ananias and Sapphira took their atonement into their own hands and inflicted on themselves a judgment never intended by our Lord.

Their sin against the Holy Spirit was to say no to his impinging influence for good. They said no when the scheme was devised and when it was exposed. Death was a natural result of uncontrollable fear and shame.

This is parabolic of our spiritual deaths. Churches die when they are made up of Christians who persistently say no to the Holy Spirit and yes to the negative, devisive, critical influences of Satan.

The question asked on the Resurrection morning can also be asked of the church. Why do you seek the living among the dead? Some of us do die inch by inch by playing at little games. We die a little each time we resist growth in Christ. To feel guilty and be guilty are two very different things.

The church exists to heal both: one with assurance and the other with exposure. God can do wonderful things with a broken heart if we will give him the pieces. That's the one thing Ananias would not do.

E. Stanley Jones once said, "I laid at Christ's feet a self of which I was ashamed, couldn't control, and couldn't live with; and to my glad astonishment he took that self, remade it, consecrated it to kingdom purposes, and gave it back to me, a self I can now live with gladly and joyously and comfortably." He learned what Proverbs 10:17 should have taught Ananias, "Anyone willing to be corrected is on the pathway to life. Anyone refusing has lost his chance" (The Living Bible). "The Christian church is the only society in the world," wrote Charles Morrison, "in which membership is based upon the qualification that the candidate shall be unworthy of membership."

The other day a man wrote me and said, "That church is filled with hypocrites!" I wrote back, "That's true, and its saving grace is that some of them know it. Come join us; there's always room for one more!"

A pastor of a church in the highlands of Scotland tried everything to revive the people and infuse the joy of Christ. He was resisted at every turn. Then one Sunday he placed an open casket in the chancel in front of the communion table. In it he carefully placed a mirror. Then he preached the church's funeral service. Afterward the people filed by the casket and looked in. Each one saw his own face!

Churches die when their members are no longer growing and adventuring. Whenever we pretend to spiritual power which we no longer have, whenever we refuse to allow Christ to change us, whenever we refuse his influence of love for each other, whenever we seek to keep the church bland and unchallenging, we begin to die. But most of all, whenever we see ourselves as we are and refuse to admit our need for Christ's forgiveness and new beginning, we miss the wonder of his grace, and Satan wins the day!

Edwin Markham's *Parable of the Builders* gives us a conclusion to what I have tried to say. There was a very rich man who owned great expanses of land. One day he walked over the hillsides and surveyed all that he owned. He saw a lovely sun-drenched hilltop below the hovel cottage of his carpenter. He went to the carpenter and said, "I have plans for a lovely home on the sunny hill. I want you to build a house there. I want you to build it good and strong. Employ the best workmen, use the best materials, for I want it to be a good house."

Then the rich man went away. The carpenter began to build the house. But as he proceeded, he decided to cut costs and pocket the difference. He built the house of inferior materials and poor workmanship. He thought he had outsmarted the owner.

When the rich man returned, he told him that he had finished the house with the best he could find and do.

"Good," said the owner, "I am glad that it is a good house. I have intended all along to give it to you. The house is yours!"

The carpenter was shocked, "Oh, if I had only known that I was building the house for myself."

Ananias didn't know that either. What about you?

CHAPTER 11

The Charismatic Communicator

A charismatic person is contagious. The grace-gifts he has received are not for himself, but for the world and the needs of people. Charisma is not for our enjoyment but for God's deployment. We exist to share the life we have been given with others.

I want to celebrate that life with you. I believe that is what authentic evangelism is—a celebration of life! The term "life" is used thirty-six times in the New Testament as a synonym for our Lord and the Christian faith. It is one of the great names given our Lord; it is used by him to describe who he is and what he came to do; it is a composite term to dramatize what happens to a person in relationship to him; and it is a designation of a new level of existence we share with each other. Evangelism is celebration of life; life as Christ lived it is the message of evangelism; life as he lives it in us is the might of evangelism; life as we communicate it to others is the method of evangelism. Living this life without reservation in all of our relationships, celebrating the Lord of Life in all things, and evangelism (the sharing of life) take place with power and contagion naturally as a result.

The admonition of the angel to the apostles released from prison encompasses the commission, the content, and the challenge of authentic evangelism. "Go and stand in the temple and speak to the people all the words of this life" (Acts 5:20). The New English Bible catches even more of the verve of the imperative: "Go and take your place in the temple and speak to the people and tell them about this new life and all that it means."

But for a simple definition of evangelism and for a text for relational evangelism which is truly incarnational, ecological, and serendipitous, I like the Good News for Modern Man: "Go and tell the people all about this new life."

Press your ear to the New Testament; listen to the Apostolic preaching; observe the church alive; behold the aftermath of Pentecost; feel the power of the Living Christ picking up his ministry where he left off at the ascension—life. That's the dominant theme, the message that turned the world upside down. They told the people *all* about this new life. But the life they preached was validated by the life they lived. New Testament evangelism was the communication of life. Paul put it all together when he said, "What is life? For me it is Christ!"

It was Pentecost which set afire the dry fagots of the memory of the life Christ lived and the message about life he preached. The Holy Spirit was Christ alive—not a sad memory, a historical figure, and unattainable challenge—but the Living Lord himself. He was no longer just the example of life which they had experienced as disciples, among them or around them, but now he was the power for this life in them. He was the life he imparted—indwelling, intimate, immediate, and initiative. That's what made the difference. Christ said:

"I am the bread of life"; "I am the way, the truth, and life"; "Within you shall spring up rivers of living water"; "I am the resurrection and the life . . . he who believes in me . . . shall live, and whoever lives and believes in me shall never die." He also said, "I shall make my home in you."

And now it was true! Go and tell the people *all* about this life. When we study the magnetic evangelism which took place after Pentecost we know what J. B. Phillips meant when he said that translating Acts was like rewiring an old house with the current turned on! We become charged by the essential message they proclaimed, electrified by the life they exposed, empowered by the relationships they lived. The defeated, discouraged, disheartened men of the upper room became the contagious communicators of the very life of Christ. Surely, if we are to rediscover an authentic evangelism for our time, if each of us is to be set afire for creative evangelism, we must return to the upper room both to hear again Christ's *charter* and *strategy* for evangelism recorded for us in John 15 and then stay on until we experience the reality of that plan in the power unleashed at Pentecost in that room fifty days later.

No picture could more vividly catch the mood I sense in the church today in America than the disciples gathered around the Lord, afraid, uncertain, confused. We deperately need to learn again what they learned about life on Passover and then to receive the life they experienced on Pentecost. When we consider both together we have the secret and the strength of charismatic evangelism. It is only a combination of the two which will prepare us to fulfill the admonition of the angel, "Go and tell the people all about this life." We, too, are imprisoned by the shackles of our own reserve, the manacles of our own ambivalence, the bars of our own impatience. Go share life? We cannot share what we do not have.

We are like the little boy who was challenged by a social worker to explain why his parents did not teach him to read. "Sir," he replied, "you cannot give what you ain't got, any more than you can go back to where you've never been!" Only what we are in the process of discovering will ever be exciting to anyone else.

On that night before he was crucified, Jesus' mind was on the future. The little band of men was his strategy. He chose a familiar image from the life of Israel to communicate the extension of his incarnation in relational evangelism. The image of Israel as the vineyard of the Lord was familiar to them, his parables had often referred to the idea. Now he boldly gives them a promise, a warning, a hope, a reason for being. "I am the vine, you are the branches." "Apart from me you can do nothing." "Abide in me and I in you." "Ask whatever you would." "This is how my Father's glory is shown: by your bearing much fruit." "Love one another as I have loved you." "You did not choose me; I chose you and appointed you to go and bear much fruit, the kind of fruit that endures." "This is my command—love one another."

The whole passage speaks of relationships, new relationships with Christ, with each other, with the world. And the purpose of it all was that we bear fruit, the fruit of his character imprinted in our nature, the fruit of communion with one another as we love as he loved us, the fruit of reproduction in others of the life we have found, the fruit that endures, changed lives which are stabilized in a transformed environment in society.

The note of prevenience, beforehand love—grace, which we can neither earn nor attain by effort—pervades this delineation of the extension of the incarnation in charismatic evangelism.

The focal point of Jesus' charter of relational evangelism

is in the prevenient commission: "You did not choose me; I chose you and appoint you to go and bear much fruit." How amazing! The call to be reproductive in communicating the life they had found was not dependent on them. Our Lord wants us to realize that it is not our adequacy or even our potential, but only his call and commission which qualifies us. This is the first essential of effective evangelism. We are not worthy, and shall never be. Before we were ready, prepared, capable, adequate, Christ called us and appointed us. That's the core of the gospel—"even while we were yet sinners."

Exactly! Jesus Christ intercedes for us and says, "I lived for you. I spoke the Word for you, I died for you. I was raised up for you. I am here now for you. You belong to me! You did not choose me, I chose you!"

> "Let me no more my comfort draw
>   From my frail hold on Thee,
> In this alone rejoice,
>   Thy mighty grasp on me."

The confusion of our minds must be broken through so that we can begin to see things as they are—Christ as he really is, ourselves as we really are. The liberating revelation must be such that at one time it shows us the truth and makes it possible for us to be honest about it. Prevenient evangelism begins with that. We know that Christ has called us, appointed us, and we belong to him in spite of what we have been or are.

This is the source of the winsome freedom which becomes the attractive ambience of our evangelism. We become concerned to share life with others, not because we must but because we may, not to justify ourselves but because we cannot remain silent about a life which has healed us and made us whole.

Therefore, we have been called for a purpose. That is to bear fruit. Jesus clarifies the essential nature of evangelism: it is to bear fruit. He uses the profound image of the vine and the branch and gives a liberating secret about the source of the life we are called to communicate. I believe that the fruit he seeks us to bear is in the reproduction of our faith in others. He is decisive in telling us that there are two kinds of branches: the one bears fruit and is pruned to bear more fruit; the other bears no fruit and is cut off and burned. The disciples knew about vines and branches. They knew about the drastic pruning process which was essential to the production of fruit. Outside the temple in Jerusalem there was a gigantic golden vine over the entrance to the sanctuary to remind the worshipers that Israel was the branch of the vine. It is in this context that he gave the secret of fruitful evangelism. He is the vine; only in contact with him do we receive the power to bear fruit. I remember the painful experience I had discovering this for myself some years ago.

I was a cut-flower Christian. I knew it; my fear was that soon others would know it. The gray grimness of self-generated piety was already on the petals of the withering bloom of my Christian life. I was wilting under the strain of seeking to produce the fruit of the Christian life while cut from the root of power. I was physically tired, emotionally spent, discouraged at my own attempts to be an adequate man for others and for God. I was filled with strain, not strength, trying, not trusting, willful, not willing. I preached the gospel with vigor but no cutting edge; I was witnessing to others about the victory of Christ, but felt defeated by my own lack of results in living what I shared; I gave leadership to others and at the same time was not being led by the inner direction of the Spirit.

I had the Elijah complex. I worked for God, his cause, his

purposes, and suddenly felt grim and determined, rather than gracious and dynamic. I felt alone, as if I had to do something for God. "I, even I only am left!" The stench of my own human heat and activity nauseated me. I had given my life to Christ and begun a life of activity for him. I worked for him and had missed the secret of allowing him to work in me. I had spent more time talking about him than talking to him; more time meeting with others about what we ought to do for him than meeting him and listening to the Word of God; more time organizing activity for him than in allowing him to organize my ambitious but ambivalent inner life. I was eccentric—away from the center in him. I had leaped upon the stallion of discipleship and was riding off in all directions.

It was during a summer study leave many summers ago that I had an experience which reoriented and redirected my life. I was busy preparing for the year ahead. I read and wrote, planned and dreamed. Then, like Elijah, I was overcome with the immensity of the task and the problem of communicating the power of Christ to individuals and enabling the church to be responsible. I was aware of the major personal, interpersonal, and social problems my people faced and were defeated by in the skirmishes of life. About that time I became convinced of the injustice in our society and the inability of the church to attack these problems with creative power. I saw the cancer of irrelevant piety eating at the vitality of the church.

I leaned back from my work. I felt a great wave of discouragement. The very people to whom I was preaching could change these social and personal problems. The impotency I felt in them was within myself. People marched before my mind's eye, and the reluctance and resistance of traditional agnostic, religious Christians mocked my lack of power. Could the church as I knew it, the bland Christians I served, change and salt the tasteless, troubled world? I pictured spastic churchmen, families deadlocked in conflict, pious church organizations playing church. At the same time I saw a sea of faces needing the love and forgiveness of Christ and a sick world needing the justice and power of the gospel.

In the midst of the anguish, I cried out loud a prayer which came from my deepest need: Oh, God! Help me to know what to say, do, be, to set your people free!

The answer was not long in coming. The same Lord who had waited patiently for me to run out of the steam of my own efforts was there. His answer to my prayer came in three ways.

My scripture study for that day was in the passage we are considering here. The words cut into the scar tissue of my own efforts to heal myself. The words burned on the page. I tried to get hold of them and then they had hold of me! Suddenly I was one with those disciples in the upper room. My mood was the same as theirs. They had been with Christ long enough to catch a vision of what life could be. Now they feared the immensity of the task without his power. And there it was, as if the words had been spoken and recorded just for me. "Apart from me, you can do nothing." That's just what I needed to learn again.

I had missed the liberating secret for charismatic evangelism. The Christian life was not just following Jesus, seeking to do what he would do or trying to work for him or bringing others to him. The secret was: Abide in me, and I in you. Contact with him, that was the answer. What I had tried to do was live the Christian life on my own strength. I was never meant to do that. I was to be a container and transmitter of the living Lord. The message of the indwelling Lord began to dawn upon me. I leafed through the pages of the New Testament to find confirmation of the reality which had always been there, but I had missed. There it was, summarized in Paul's experience: Christ in you, the hope of glory. Christ alive in you! That is the source of the power, the excitement, the adventure of the new life!

At the same time, I was reading the biography of Hudson Taylor, the founder of the China Inland Mission. Like me, Taylor had struggled to get more of Christ in his life. He prayed, agonized, fasted, made resolutions, read the Bible, but the serenity, vitality, and power he sought eluded him. One day, he received a letter from another missionary. The last paragraph hit him between the eyes; "Not striving to have faith," it read, "or to increase our faith, but looking to the faithful one seems all that we need. An abiding in the loved one entirely, from time and eternity." Hudson Taylor was amazed at his own blindness. "I'll strive no more," he said. "It was all a mistake to try to get the fullness out of Christ. He has promised to abide in me. I am a part of him. Each one of us is a limb of his body, a branch of his vine." After that day, people noticed a change in Hudson Taylor. He labored, he prayed, he disciplined himself harder than ever, but not with a sense of strain and agony. He now radiated a magnetism of love and joy, for he was no longer a man who struggled, but a man who was being used.

Yes, that was it. I had been filled with strain and struggle but no freedom, and the Spirit met me at the point of my need. As I sat there in quiet prayer, I felt the gentle rain of mercy watering the parched places of my spirit. I knew what Isaiah had discovered. There was a difference between carrying God and being carried by God. When he observed the pagan rituals and watched the people carrying about their idols, the Lord spoke to him and said, "And even to your old age, I will carry you." I felt the lift of the burden to be adequate and felt truly free for the first time in my life. I felt like Jacob limping away from an encounter with God, exclaiming, "This is the Lord's doing, and it is marvelous in our eyes." He had been waiting all along for me to run out of my own self-generated effort so that I could learn that his strength was sufficient for me. That was the first taste of Christian freedom for me, and it whetted a voracious hunger which has never been completely satisfied.

The third aspect of our Lord's answer was incarnated in a person. A friend was given to me that summer who had the capacity to listen with love. He drew me out. I told him essentially what I have told you here. Then he lowered the scalpel of loving surgery on the things which made me uncomfortable in the Lord's presence. I faced with him the relationships and memories which debilitated my freedom and effectiveness. Then in his presence I asked Christ to live his life in and through me.

The truth which became a reality in my experience is what Paul explained in Galatians 2:20: "It is no longer I who live, but Christ who lives in me; and the life I now live in the flesh I live by faith in the Son of God, who loved me and gave himself for me." I found that my human nature is to be an agency by which Christ can reveal himself. Christ had become the center of my being. Attention was now centered on him and witnessing was transformed from conceptual idealism to concrete sharing of what Christ was doing in the down-to-earth, natural, normal, everyday things of life. Christ had created my "self" to be the vessel to contain and communicate his life. Before, my life was a strenuous effort to do what was right. Now I knew that by myself I could not do what was right. But he could do within me, what I could not do on my own. That's when the adventure began for me. I was constantly amazed at what he could do with my humanity and my circumstances. Everything takes on new significance as the content of witness about the new life. This is where deep contact with others occurs—when we are free to share out of the discoveries in the problems and frustrations of our humanity.

What a difference there was in my life and work when I returned home. Now my humanity was not to be perfected in order to be deserving of the Lord, but it became the raw material which Christ used to communicate what he could do with a life put at his disposal. I no longer felt that I had to perfect myself for him, but now yielded my clay vessel to contain him. My inadequacy, failure, lack of love or patience now became the very things through which I could identify with others and share what Christ was doing. Instead of trying to reform my humanity, I began to enjoy it. The focus of my life was not how to be good enough to deserve his love, for that is to keep the attention on me. I began to think much more about Christ and less about my perfection. The result, inadvertently, was that I became more and more the person I was created to enjoy being.

This experience is updated daily. In new challenges, like that of being called to a new position which requires gifts and wisdom beyond me, I am forced to return to the same discovery again. I am inadequate—always have been and always will be—but Christ who lives in me is more than adequate.

"Whoever remains in me, and I in him, will bear much fruit." What Christ seems to be saying is that he is the evangelist. Paul caught the essence of this in Ephesians 2:10. He talks about walking in the things God has prepared. In other words, the things we do in obedience to him are already prepared. They are prepared in the sense not only that he tells us what to do, but that he is doing them through us. Christ is at work! Luke talks through Acts about the things Jesus began to do and teach. Luke concludes with the end of the historical ministry of Jesus of

Nazareth and the Acts of the Apostles begins with the things the resurrected, living, indwelling Christ continued to do and teach through the apostles.

There is one evangel, one evangelist; our task in charismatic evangelism is to be channels for Christ himself, to do his work with people. We are to communicate the dynamic that Christ is Lord of all. Our task is not to force people to make him their Lord. He is that already. Faith is accepting what has always been true. We are to help people accept the love which has been there all along. In becoming a Christian, we accept the fact that we are loved and forgiven and open ourselves to his living Spirit.

"If you remain in me, and I in you, ask whatever you will." This is the source of guidance for prevenient evangelism. Prayer begins with our Lord. He places within us the desire to communicate his love to some particular person. When we ask him, it is not our task to convince him of a person's need. He knows that already and has prompted us to pray. Our concern is to be so deeply engrossed in moment-by-moment prayer that we sense the movement of his guiding Spirit to these people who are next on his agenda for us to share his life. How absurd our compulsive evangelism seems when we think of it. We do not have to press God into loving a person. That is true already. But what we do need is to get into the rhythm of his guidance so that we are ready for those whom he has made ready.

"This is how my Father is glorified, that you bear much fruit." The glory of the Lord is the manifestation of the Lord. He is manifested in the fruit he produces through us. The fruit he produces *in* us is what he wants to produce *through* us. I believe the fruit of the indwelling Christ is ministry to other people who receive a taste of the new life in relationship with us. When the Lord lives in us he manifests himself by making us more like him in our character; we meet him in communion with others where he is the source of unity and fellowship; we communicate with others to reproduce in them the reality we have found; and we join with him in his work in society to bring justice and freedom for all men.

By the power of the indwelling Lord we are called to make a gigantic leap to catch the swinging pendulum. Suddenly we realize that the pendulum is not swinging between personal faith and social action. It's movement is not a yin-yang, ping-pong alternation between two polarities, but is encircling, encompassing. It moves quadrilaterally. Christ himself is the pendulum, and he swings us about to include what life in him must always include: personal union with him, active involvement in remedial relationships in *koinonia*, dynamic concern to share grace with others who do not know him, and persistent concern for society and its sick structures.

Whenever we present one of these apart from all the rest we lead people into heresy and ineffectiveness. The danger of our time is that there are those who want to make the gospel only one of these. Once again we need to respond to the angel who releases us from the prison of singularity, or even debilitating duality, and says, "Go tell the people *all* about the new life."

During the past ten years the church has been struggling to learn how to run on a two-legged gospel. We have limped on one leg of either personal faith or social action. Look at the horrendous task it has been to mobilize the people of God to care about society! But the same reprogramming of the mind of the church which was required for that is now necessary for a missing ingredient we have forgotten: any person who accepts Christ without at the same time accepting the challenge of communicating his faith to others will soon become a self-centered, sick Christian.

Personal evangelism is not a luxury or a calling of particular Christians. It is an essential dimension of life in Christ.

I want to talk to you about your grandchildren in Christ. If we cannot point to someone who is alive in Christ because of the life and witness of someone whom we have helped into the new life, then we have missed the essential nature of relational evangelism. We are to communicate the life in Christ in such a way that people see that sharing what they have found is an undeniable necessity to coming and staying alive in the relationship with him.

Charismatic evangelism is entering into deep caring relationships with people in which the new life is modeled and mediated. It is communicating life in the "crucible of identification." This is what Jesus meant when he reminded them of the way he had loved them. He pointed to his death as the supreme act of self-giving. He has called us to die to our own selfish plans and schedules, privacy, and comfort. "The greatest love a man can have for his friends is to give his life for them." That's the painful challenge of true evangelism. It is person-centric involvement in the context of total concern for a person's life. It is not hit and run conceptualism in which we blast into a person's life, spew out theoretical concepts of salvation, wrench a decision from him, and move on to new ego trips. The issue of our time is the issue of finding ways of communicating with people who have heard the language and traditions of religion and have bypassed them as irrelevant to their lives. A freshness, a charismatic sparkle is needed if we are to reach the pagan, post-Christian world in which we live.

John Masefield said it:

> "The bolted door had broken in
> I knew that I had done with sin
> I knew that Christ had given me birth
> To brother all the souls on earth."

Jesus' strategy of evangelism was for us to be to each other what He has been to us. He loved his disciples in the way he had been loved by the Father. Now they were to love each other and the people he gave them, just as he had loved them. Amy Carmichael once said:

> "No wound? No scar?
>   Yet, as the Master so shall the servant be
> And pierced are the feet that follow Me;
>   But thine are whole: Can he have followed far
> Who has no scar?"

We hear a lot about ecology these days. The word means the interdependence of all species and the natural world upon each other. Evangelism is ecological. God has made us interdependent for the experience of his love. We are responsible for other people and their relationship to the Lord.

Authentic evangelism is loving, listening, caring, and sharing. The great gift of the indwelling Christ is the capacity of accepting, affirming love. It's the delight a person comes to feel about himself when he is with us. This is the ambience in which a person can see himself as he is and what could happen to him if he allowed God to manage his life. When people are loved, they are free to talk about themselves, their dreams, hopes, fears, frustrations, and disappointments. That's where remedial listening comes in. If we truly trust that Christ is present and his love is already at work in a person, we can listen lovingly as he talks about his life.

Listen, can you hear the plea of the people around you? Seneca echoed it long ago and died by his own hand: "Listen to me for a day, an hour, a moment, Lest I expire in my terrible wilderness, My lonely silence! O, God, is there no one to listen?"

When Helen Keller spoke of her soul's sudden awakening, she said, "Somehow the mastery of language was revealed to me, I knew that water meant that wonderful, cool something that was flowing over my hand." Ann Sullivan had matched sounds with feelings. That's what evangelism is all about: identifying the relationship of the deep inner needs of people with the refreshing healing of God's love. When people sense what Christ has done in us, they can feel what it might be like for them. Not concepts alone, but communion; not rationalizing, but relationalizing—that's evangelism!

I believe that our Lord has called us together here to evangelize us so that we can evangelize the world. One of the most exciting things which I see in our time of history is what our Lord is doing in the lives of church people who have been agnostic Christians for years. There is a fantastic ferment in the body of Christ today, and I believe it is happening through people who have come to a fresh experience of our Lord's indwelling power.

Our great need is to tarry in the upper room for Pentecost. It was not just the great commission which motivated the evangelization of the world. As a matter of fact, it wasn't until some time later that Peter, and later Paul, got around to living out the charge to evangelize the nations. If Jesus' commission had been enough, they would have sprung into action immediately at the Ascension. Not so!

Take the experience of the Apostle Peter, trace all through the New Testament, and you realize what was necessary for Jesus Christ to do in order to finally make a quadrilateral evangelist. Jesus began when he called Peter from his fishing nets, but he didn't leave him there. He confronted him on the road to Caesarea Philippi and said, "Who do men say that I am?" And Simon was able to answer, "Thou art the Christ." But he didn't leave him there

for that conceptual conviction was not enough. He said,
"I'm going to give you the keys of the kingdom, change your
name, give you a new perspective and power." And then he
said, "Go and storm the gates of Hell." And I believe that
that's an essential dimension of what evangelism is all
about. Storming the gates of personal, interpersonal, and
social hell. But he didn't leave him there. Later he said,
"Satan will want to sift you like wheat, but I am praying for
you." But he didn't leave him there. He came to Peter
beside the sea after the resurrection. For threefold denial
there was an opportunity for a remedial, threefold
affirmation. "Simon, do you love me?" Note carefully the
word Simon Peter used to respond: "Lord, you know that I
am your friend." Now observe Jesus' gracious descent to
Peter's cautious reserve to put verbal arms of love around
the equivocating apostle: "Are you really my friend?
Then feed my lambs, tend my sheep." All recall to person-
centric evangelism in the context of physical and
spiritual need!

But he did not leave him there! He did not leave him to
suffer with a guilt-producing admonition, a vision of life he
had no power to live or share. He returned, and came to live
his postresurrection life in the apostle so that wherever
Peter went, the power of Jesus Christ moved out. This
cracked rock was brought back again and again to what he
had heard there in the upper room on Passover. "Apart from
me, you can do nothing." But the Lord didn't leave him
there. He had to change his prejudices about the Gentile
world and lift his expectation level to include people he had
been taught to negate since he was a child. Like a person
with a distorted muscle system, he had to be repatterned
with the impulses of the inclusive mind of Christ. The Lord
gave him the vision of the fruit lowered down from heaven
and the ministry to Cornelius. Only after years, Peter finally

got around to Jesus' admonition to share the gospel with the whole world and with all nations.

Is it any wonder that the Living Christ has such a time with all of us? He will not leave us wherever we are. He will not leave us in our little corner with a segment of the life.

I think many of us are like Apollos, the man who had everything, but needed someone. Apollos is the patron saint of many of us in the church today. He was fervent in spirit, but not filled with the Spirit. He had training, skill, oratorical effectiveness, theological clarity, but no power to change lives. But, also like him, I believe that we long for what happened to him after encounter with Priscilla and Aquilla. There's an effective model of relational evangelism! They began with affirmation, what B.F. Skinner would call reinforcement, and they were supportive of his efforts and gifts, but, having won the right to be heard, they pointed the way to life by the Holy Spirit, Christ the indwelling contemporary. The result was a harvest of new life. I have always felt that the difference was in the fact that Apollos stopped trying to follow and proclaim Jesus as a historical figure, the Christ of Israel, and allowed the living Lord to dwell in him. I think that he became much more personal as he talked about the result of the relationship of the living Christ for the relationships of his own life. People were no longer impressed with Apollos, but infused with the living Christ.

St. Augustine was on target when he portrayed the entire Christian enterprise as that in which one loving heart sets another on fire. The gift of the Holy Spirit is the gift of fire—illumination, warmth, dynamic power for the communication of love to others. William Barclay said, "A witness is essentially a man who speaks from firsthand knowledge. He is a man who says, 'This is true and I know it.' He is a man who knows from personal experience that

what he says is true; and it is impossible to stop a man like
that because it is impossible to stop the truth."

This is the kind of witness our world desperately needs
today. I have come to believe that the sin against the Holy
Spirit of which Jesus spoke as the unforgivable sin is
refusing to be a channel for the Spirit to communicate his
love and life to others through us. Evangelism is not a
luxury of a select few or the particular calling of an
especially gifted few. It is essential for everyone who would
remain alive in Christ. If we were meant to be contagious
communicators of life, the greatest of all sins is to be
ineffective in this reason we were born. The people around
us need Christ more than they need anything or anyone
else. Sin is the thing which keeps us from being
communicators of God's power. We sin against the Holy
Spirit through reserve, embarrassment, the need to be
liked, or petulant privacy. Whatever keeps us from being
willing to enter into deep caring relationships in which we
are able to reach the jugular vein of a person's need—that is
sin. Whatever causes us to resist the opportunity to invite a
man to turn his problem, and with it his life, over to Christ
is quenching the Holy Spirit. The Holy Spirit is the divine
energy of love seeking to break through to people. He never
closes our heart. He tears it open constantly for the sake of
others.

Remember Screwtape's word to Wormwood about how to
destroy the saints? "Keep his mind on the inner life . . . .
keep his mind off the elementary duties by directing it to
the most advanced and spiritual ones. Aggregate that most
useful human characteristic, the neglect of the obvious."

The neglect of the obvious! We wonder why we miss the
essential calling of every Christian to be a life changer, to be
an enabler of new life? The sulphurous smell of hell is
nothing compared with the vile odor emitted by stale grace

gone putrid—the grace of God corrupted by spiritual vanity. There is no vanity like that of a Christian who believes that God has called and loved him in forgiving acceptance and that he has no responsibility to share that with others. A silent Christian is a brash contradiction of terms!

But there are discernible reasons why this satisfaction with stale grace is tolerated, even encouraged, in the church today. I believe it is because we have presented the gospel as a private affair. Many of us as leaders resist the central calling to be one-to-one liberators of people. Clergy teach, preach, counsel, and administrate, but many feel incapable of helping one person find the power of God in his life. Therefore, life-changing is not an essential ingredient of our presentation of the gospel. We reproduce ourselves in our people. When we present the Christian faith to people apart from the necessity of being reproductive, we lead people down a dead end. The result is that we may be able to sustain spiritual vigor in a parish for a time, but it soon diminishes because people have not learned that communicating their faith to individuals is not a luxury but an undeniable responsibility. Our calling is not to produce churchmen to keep our program going, but to produce a reproductive laity—people who are ministers in the world, able to be vulnerable, open, free in sharing what Christ has and is doing in their lives and able to lead people to the realization of the love and forgiveness and adventure of Christ. Without this the church, church work, religious activity, and self-propelled, self-justifying piety will become the diminutive gods which become lord of people's lives instead of Jesus Christ as Lord.

I remember talking to a friend who was bogged down in his Christian life. He was locked on dead center, parched in a dry spell, ineffective and with little sense of the joy of Christ in his life. As we talked, I was aware that he could point to no one person who was alive in Christ because of his relationship with him. He was a great bird dog for sniffing out human need. I know about dozens of people for whom he cared in many costly ways. He gave his time, energy, money, and life to them. But, like a salesman who could present his product but made no sales because he could never close the deal, my friend could never help a person to surrender his life to Christ and receive the indwelling power of the Holy Spirit. When a relationship got to that point, he would bring the person to one of a number of his life-changing friends who would close the deal. I have pondered long and hard why this is so. There is a boldness lacking which can gently but firmly ask a person to trust his life to Christ's prevenient love. My friend wants it to happen, rejoices when it does through someone else, but has never had it happen through him.

Recently, I probed a bit to find out why this was persistently the case. He had grown into the Christian life through the church and had always considered himself a Christian. He was faithful in living out the mandate for social action, had been vigilant in his own radical obedience, had been jailed for his convictions in a demonstration for social justice. But the missing quality was that he was impersonal about his own life. He listened to people, cared about their needs, but was silent when it came to telling about what Christ was doing in his own struggles and strains as a person. He could hear out a person with a troubled marriage, but could never tell them what Christ had done in his own. He has never made a complete and unreserved surrender of his privacy to Christ and has not asked the Holy Spirit to use his own experience as the data of his witness to others. At the core of it is a gigantic arrogance and pride. He really believes that by his example people will somehow find what he has found. Not so! He can lead people only as far as he has gone himself.

I know a couple who have loved Christ for years. But there is a new power in their lives. They have always been effective leaders, rooted in a conservative, biblical faith and involved in the life of the church. There's something fresh and vital about them now. Their experience of the Holy Spirit has given them gifts for ministry with people in need which constantly amazes me. They are broken bread and poured-out wine for those in trouble. The wife teaches a Bible class in her home on weekday mornings, her husband is involved with dozens of people at the university where he teaches, their evening meeting in their home is like a chapter in the book of Acts. They have a ministry with dope-addicted people, work in the prisons, and listen to people with personal problems, as well as faithful church people who long for the reality of God in their lives. Their home is a center of healing and release for people—young and old, clean and dirty, straight and square, religious and pagan, black and white, all God's people in search of life.

As I consider the major social crises in our area, I see people from the church deployed. Many of these were previously up-tight, traditional Christians who knew a great deal about "decency and order" Christianity, but now have a burning love for people and a creative indignation for the social conditions which frustrate and debilitate others. Their recent personal experience of Christ in the practical areas of their own lives has given them an excitement about Christ as the agent of change for persons and society. They have taken seriously what it means to learn how to communicate their faith to individuals and also to fight social injustice. Here again the quadralateral evangelism is being rediscovered: personal faith, in-depth *koinonia*, reproduction of faith in individuals, and creative involvement in the sores of society.

It is a joy to see people bring others to worship with them and then follow through to help their problems. The spectrum is amazing. A community leader was reached by a peer and found new life in the preparation classes. An entertainer was reached by a fellow actor. A couple whose relationship with each other and Christ was on the rocks, made a new beginning as they turned their lives over to Christ and found the secret of a new marriage. A Jewish woman who works for a network was alerted to an alternative to her emptiness by a woman who is exuberant with joy. A famous actor was led to the church by a contractor who shared his faith with him as he worked on his home. An executive confessed his faith in Christ as the result of being in a businessmen's group with some of the members. A family started a Sunday luncheon group for young adults and have reached many for Christ. A retired man gives his time and business skill to economic problems of disadvantaged. The list is endless. And that's the new kind of evangelism that I see. A new kind of cadre moving out into the world that will not be satisfied with one dimension of the gospel without all of them and will not present the gospel to anyone in a way that gives only a part of but not the whole of it.

The question is: Has our charisma made us communicators? I think we're no different from those apostles as they waited in the upper room. I believe that the church in America is out of steam; that our denominations are questing for a way to go in our time of history. I think our local churches are languishing, wondering what the next steps are. And unless I miss my guess in the basic relationships of life, there's a need for Jesus Christ to do something fresh and real right now that will change our attitude toward ourselves and toward the people in our lives. I'm sure that every one of us has blocked our Lord some place: something that is hidden; a disturbing memory down inside; a restitution that needs to be made, a reconciliation that needs to be performed; something that needs to be confessed; something that needs to be healed. And that's the reason that we've come. Not to get a new clever plan of evangelism, but to get healed ourselves! Because once that happens, there will be no containing us because then the excitement of Jesus Christ will be real for each of us personally. I believe that unless someone in the last week has pressed us to know the reason for the excitement that's in us, then we're not living life as it was meant to be.

That's the challenge of charismatic evangelism. We are grace-gifted people with a purpose. It is to go and tell others all about the new life.